W9-BBU-386

Analytical
Review

Analytical Review

A Guide To Evaluating Financial Statements

Edward Blocher, Ph.D., CPA, CMA
University of North Carolina

John J. Willingham, Ph.D., CPA,
Peat, Marwick, Mitchell & Company

McGraw-Hill Book Company
New York   St. Louis
San Francisco   Auckland
Bogotá   Hamburg
Johannesburg   London
Madrid   Mexico   Montreal
New Delhi   Panama   Paris
São Paulo   Singapore   Sydney
Tokyo   Toronto

Library of Congress Cataloging in Publication Data

Blocher, Edward J.
    Analytical review.

    Includes index.
    1. Auditing, Analytical review.   I. Willingham, John J.   II. Title.
HF5667.B536   1985   657'.3   84-7172
ISBN 0-07-005912-8

1234567890   DOC/DOC   8910987654

ISBN 0-07-005912-8

The editors for this book were Martha Jewett and William B. O'Neal, the designer was Dennis Sharkey, and the production supervisor was Reiko F. Okamura. It was set in Baskerville by *Byrd* Data Imaging Group.
Printed and bound by R. R. Donnelley & Sons Company

The material quoted in Appendixes One, Two, and Three reflects the unfortunate absence of personal pronouns in the English language which mean "he or she" and other such inflections. Traditionally, "he," "his," etc., have been used generically in such instances. This is the case in these appendixes, and such usage should be assumed to refer both to women and to men.

contents

CHAPTER FIVE
THE REASONABLENESS TEST   99

CHAPTER SIX
USING ANALYTICAL REVIEW FOR
SELECTED ACCOUNTS   115

CHAPTER SEVEN
THE FINAL ANALYTICAL REVIEW   139

CHAPTER EIGHT
ANALYTICAL REVIEW GUIDANCE   145

APPENDIX ONE
SAS 23, "ANALYTICAL REVIEW
PROCEDURES"   163

APPENDIX TWO
SELECTED PARAGRAPHS FROM *SSARS 1*,
"COMPILATION AND REVIEW OF
FINANCIAL STATEMENTS"   169

APPENDIX THREE
SELECTED PARAGRAPHS FROM *SAS 36*,
"REVIEW OF INTERIM FINANCIAL
INFORMATION"   173

APPENDIX FOUR
REGRESSION ANALYSIS IN ANALYTICAL
REVIEW   179

INDEX   191

preface

This book will help auditors to use analytical review most effectively. It can be used by both external and internal auditors as a guide and a reference for selecting, performing, and interpreting the results of analytical review. There are a number of audit uses for analytical review—the audit engagement, the review engagement, the internal audit assignment, the preacquisition review, and many others.

Analytical review is the name for a variety of techniques the auditor can use to assess the risk of undetected error in financial records. Analytical review provides substantive audit evidence of the fairness of the reported amount, based on the auditor's analysis of the relationships between financial and operating data for the auditee. It differs from detail audit tests in that it typically requires very little auditor time or resources. Especially when the risk and materiality for an account are low, analytical review can be a very efficient and effective method for obtaining audit evidence.

Many auditors feel that the full potential of analytical review has not been realized. A common explanation for this is a general lack of understanding of what analytical review is, how it is properly applied, and how much it should be relied upon. It is precisely this lack of understanding which has motivated us to write this book, and we have prepared it with these concerns in mind.

In odd contrast to the general lack of confidence in analytical review noted above, it is used widely in audit practice. Thus, the objective of the book is to show how the available well-known techniques can be used most effectively, rather than merely to describe an assortment of review techniques which are already familiar to the auditor.

For the more experienced auditors, our book will be an aid to getting the most benefit from the use of the analytical procedures they are now using. Also, it will help the experienced auditor to identify new applications of analytical review. For the less experienced auditor, the book will be useful for training and as a reference to assist in resolving the day-to-day questions which come up in the audit or review engagement. We feel the book will be especially useful for the inexperienced auditor, since the effectiveness of analytical review is very dependent on the auditor's knowledge and experience, more so than for other audit procedures.

As our focus is on guidance for the well-known analytical review procedures, our approach in the book is to provide a nontechnical presentation of these well-known and easy-to-apply methods. However, because regression analysis is becoming more common in analytical review applications, we discuss it in a nontechnical manner in the book, and supplement this with the more technical aspects of regression in an appendix.

The basis for our suggestions and guidance contained in this book is our research in recent years of auditors' analytical review judgments. Also, we have used the results from other researchers, who are cited frequently throughout the book. This research has identified the judgment biases and mistakes made by auditors when planning and using analytical review. The research has also provided some preliminary evidence on the relative effectiveness of various analytical review procedures. Our book makes this important research information available to the auditor in a nontechnical, easy-to-read form.

Chapter 1 presents some basic information about the nature of analytical review and its role in the external audit, the internal audit, the review engagement, and related types of engagements. Chapter 2 describes the elements of inherent risk and the means for analyzing and evaluating it by analytical review. *Inherent risk* is the risk that a material error will occur in the accounting records, apart from the influence of the internal control system or the auditor's testing. Chapters 3 through 5 then deal with the three common analytical review procedures—trend analysis, ratio analysis, and the reasonableness test, respectively. Chapter 6 explains the approach we suggest for selecting an analytical review procedure for each account. Certain procedures are expected to be more effective for specific accounts, and other procedures are more effective for other accounts. Also, there is a discussion of the use of analytical review for choosing which of many branches, or "sites," to test, given that the auditor is not able to examine all sites. Chapter 7 briefly describes the objectives and procedures for the conduct of analytical review at the end of the audit engagement, as part of the final review. Chapter 8 includes our suggestions for incorporating work sheet decision aids and other explicit forms of guidance into the review procedure to enhance the effectiveness of auditor usage of analytical review. The appendixes include selected relevant portions of the *Statements on Auditing Standards,* plus the somewhat technical presentation of regression analysis. We hope you find the book to be thoroughly interesting and useful.

Edward Blocher
John J. Willingham

chapter
one

The Uses
of Analytical
Review

A continuing concern for auditors is the choice of procedures to use in achieving audit objectives. In response to this concern, increasing attention is given to analytical review as a means for improving audit efficiency. *Analytical review* is a name for a variety of techniques for gathering audit evidence through analyses of expected relationships between an organization's operating and financial data, using ratios, trends, reasonableness tests, and related procedures. An important common characteristic of these procedures is that they require relatively little auditor time or resources. For this reason they are preferable to other audit procedures when they are sufficient to achieve the given audit objective. However, many auditors argue against increased reliance on analytical review until the profession and the individual auditor understand it much better. They point to the unexplained diversity of use for analytical review procedures among the largest firms, and to the perceived low precision of the procedures, as conditions which indicate the need for guidance before the procedures are used more extensively.

Auditors both in practice and in academia are pursuing ongoing research efforts to provide the desired improvement in our understanding of analytical review procedures. The research has two thrusts:

1. To develop new and more effective analytical review procedures

2. To discover whatever obstacles there might be for auditors in using current procedures effectively and to develop the practical forms of guidance (checklists, decision flowcharts, etc.) to address these obstacles

While both types of research are important, our primary interest is in the latter, that is, helping auditors use available methods more effectively. Moreover, we are specifically concerned with the analytical review procedures which are well known and in widespread usage, rather than with the newer mathematical and statistical methods, such as regression and time-series analysis. We feel the greatest overall benefit will come from more effective use of the well-known procedures rather than from the wider use of the new mathematical and statistical procedures.

It is not appropriate here to pursue the arguments supporting or refuting this position, as it would necessarily be a lengthy and probably inconclusive discussion. However, restricting our efforts to the well-known procedures should not limit the utility of this book for most auditors since these procedures are useful for a wide variety of audit engagements, whereas the utility of the mathematical and statistical procedures may depend on the size of the engagement, the audit history, and the availability of expertise.

OBJECTIVES OF THE BOOK

This book can be used for both instructional and reference purposes. In the first instance, it provides a comprehensive presentation of analytical review which shows the auditor how to use the procedures most effectively. To facilitate quick and lasting learning of the material, illustrations and case examples are used frequently. The focus throughout is on those well-known procedures now used in audit practice, so the terms and concepts will be familiar to most auditors. However, the presentation assumes no prior knowledge of analytical review, so the inexperienced auditor or student will find it useful as well.

Since the procedures will be familiar to most auditors, a key aspect of the approach of the book is to highlight the *obstacles* to the most effective use of these procedures. This is done by identifying and explaining the most common judgment mistakes an auditor can make in applying and interpreting the results of an analytical review procedure. This exposition is based in part on the findings of extensive research projects by ourselves and others. Generally, these mistakes involve the use of irrelevant or incomparable data in the process of assessing the reasonableness of some figure. A second aspect of the approach of the book is to develop a strategy for choosing which of the procedures should be used in analyzing a given financial statement account. Again, by reference in part to prior research, we will see that certain procedures are more effective than others for certain accounts, but that no single procedure is preferred for all accounts.

The book does not require an understanding of mathematical and statistical concepts and techniques beyond that level contained in the *Statements on Auditing Standards (SAS),* the American Institute of Certified Public Accountants guidelines to the profession. However, regression and time-series models are known to be useful in certain applications of analytical review, so a thorough presentation of how to develop and apply these statistical models is given in Appendix 4. This appendix explains the proper statistical interpretation of the models, the common mistakes in developing the models, and the conditions for which the models are most effectively applied.

In addition to the instructional objective described above, the book can be used as a reference to guide the auditor's analyses of a given account balance. This use of the book is facilitated by the inclusion of decision flowcharts, outlines, and illustrations which promptly direct the auditor's attention to the needed information.

WHO SHOULD USE THE BOOK?

The book will assist both the independent auditor and the internal auditor in selecting and in interpreting the results of analytical review procedures. Though the overall audit objectives for independent versus internal auditors differ substantially, the role which analytical review plays in the audit process for each is quite similar. That is, analytical review is used to direct the auditor's attention to those areas with the greatest potential for material misstatement, and to provide a basis for allocating effort using this indication of potential for misstatement. Both independent and internal auditors are served by these two uses of analytical review.

Examples of uses for the independent auditor: (1) The auditor might use trend analysis to assess which of a set of expense accounts has the highest potential for misstatement, or (2) use a gross profit test to assess the reasonableness of the cost-of-sales/sales relationship, relative to prior years.

Examples of uses for the internal auditor: (1) Suppose a company has several contracts with others to supply goods and services to the company per contract. The internal auditor must choose a sample of these contractors for audit on a periodic basis. An analytical review approach would be used to determine which of the contractors might have the greatest potential for error, that is, billing the company for costs not covered by the contract. (2) The internal auditor would use an analytical procedure to determine which of several branch locations of a multilocation company (for example, a bank with many offices) to audit on a periodic basis.

It is useful to distinguish the *financial audit* from the *operational* or *management audit* when considering audit objectives. The financial audit is concerned with the bona fides of the reported amounts, whereas the operational or management audit is concerned with operational efficiency and management compliance with established policies. The independent auditor is primarily associated with the financial audit; the internal auditor can be involved in either type of audit. The book is designed principally for the financial audit, where analytical review procedures are most commonly used.

WHERE ANALYTICAL REVIEW IS USED BY THE INDEPENDENT AUDITOR

Analytical review can be used by the independent auditor in a variety of situations including the conventional financial audit engagement. There are five easily identified uses:

The Financial Audit Engagement
In the financial audit, analytical review is a substantive auditing procedure which can be used to direct the auditor's attention to areas with the highest potential for material misstatement. Alternatively, it can be used to reduce the scope of other substantive tests in an audit area where risk and materiality are low and where the auditor can be satisfied by the results of the analytical review procedure. Also, it can be used as a

compensating test in lieu of tests of internal control compliance, and at the final review of the audit working papers to assess the overall reasonableness of the financial statements. The use of analytical review in the financial audit is described more fully in *SAS 23*, "Analytical Review Procedures" (Appendix 1).

The Review Engagement

A review engagement has a narrower scope than that of the financial audit. The auditor expresses only limited assurance that the financial statements do not depart materially from conformity with generally accepted accounting principles. Review procedures consist of certain inquiries and analytical procedures. See *Statements on Standards for Accounting and Review Services (SSARS) 1*, "Compilation and Review of Financial Statements" (Appendix 2).

Review of Interim Financial Information

When interim financial information is presented together with the financial statements, or is presented alone and purports to conform to the provisions of *Accounting Principles Board (APB) Opinion 28*, "Interim Financial Reporting," then certain review procedures and reporting standards apply as described in *SAS 36*, "Review of Interim Financial Information" (Appendix 3). The review procedures consist primarily of certain inquiries and analytical review. Review of internal controls and limited tests of details might also be involved.

Special Reports

For the auditor who is involved in an engagement in which scope is limited to certain elements, items, or accounts of a financial statement, the proper test procedures and reporting standards are described in *SAS 35*, "Special Reports—Applying Agreed Upon Procedures . . ." The *SAS* does not prescribe the procedures to be applied, but in practice the auditor will find it useful to apply analytical review procedures in the planning and testing phases of the engagement. Preacquisition reviews and reviews of creditors' claims are examples of this type of engagement.

Budgeting and Short-Run Financial Planning

It is apparent that the use of analytical review, which involves an understanding of financial and operating relationships, is in effect an important part of the process of short-run financial planning and budgeting. That is, projecting account balances and relationships between accounts and operating data is an integral part of both analytical review and short-run financial planning. Thus, developing an expertise in analytical review should have benefits to the independent auditor both within the audit practice and for that portion of the consulting practice which provides financial planning services for clients.

THE NATURE, TIMING, AND EXTENT OF ANALYTICAL REVIEW

Given these different uses for analytical review, we are interested in whether there should be differences in the nature, timing, and extent of analytical review for each. Also, it appears that the second, third, and fourth applications (review, interim information, and special reports, respectively) are quite similar, since all three require analytical review and inquiry to provide limited assurance that there is no material misstatement. Thus, we will use the term "review-type engagement" to refer to these collectively in the following discussion, which contrasts the nature, timing, and extent of analytical review for (1) the independent audit engagement, (2) the review-type engagement, and (3) internal auditing (the operational audit excluded).

Nature

Since independent audit, review, and internal auditing are all concerned with financial statement accounts, there is no difference in the nature of analytical review between them. That is, the risk analysis or analytical procedure would be applied in the same manner in each case.

Timing

The audit engagement has three principal phases—planning, field work, and final review. During initial planning, analytical review is used to evaluate the overall risk of the entity by considering financial liquidity and related measures of the entity's ability to maintain a going concern. The results of this evaluation are important in setting the overall scope of audit testing. In application to individual accounts, analytical review helps to direct attention to accounts which might be materially misstated, by identifying those with unusual relationships or changes relative to the prior period. Also, an analytical review procedure can be used to reduce the amount of detail testing in an account, if the auditor is satisfied that the procedure is sufficiently accurate and if the materiality and risk of the account are low. Since analytical review provides negative rather than positive assurance, this work-reducing role of analytical review requires careful judgment. When the risk or materiality of an account is high, the auditor may choose to employ a limited analytical review, or omit it entirely, and rely on detail testing.

Analytical review is also employed in the second phase of the audit—the field work. Here it is used to assist in selecting subsegments of the entity, or periods of transactions within an account, for in-depth examination. For example, it is used in selecting branch retail stores for detail work. Second, it is used in those situations where the auditor must estimate an account balance for the purpose of making an adjustment or assisting the client in making an accrual. For example, the auditor might use an analytical review approach to estimate the amount of a contingent liability.

Then in the final phase of the audit, analytical review is applied to assess the overall reasonableness of the financial statements. This review can lead to additional audit work if an account balance or relationship appears to be unreasonable.

An internal audit activity can be viewed in the same manner, except that the final review phase is generally not applicable since the internal audit is not typically intended to attest to the reasonableness of the financial statements taken as a whole. Also, it is generally not meaningful to consider phases for the review-type engagement, since it involves limited procedures which do not require extensive planning or review for overall reasonableness.

Extent

The extent of analytical review in any engagement depends on many factors—risk, materiality, cost-benefit, applicability of analytical review relative to other procedures, and so on. However, the principal factor which determines the extent of analytical review to be used in independent audit, review, and internal audit engagements is the availability and effectiveness of substitutable procedures. In the audit engagement, tests of details are the substitute for analytical review, whereas in review engagements the principal substitute is inquiry. The internal auditor may use both inquiry and tests of details in addition to the analytical review.

Thus, the chief difference between independent audit, review, and internal audit engagements is the *extent* of the use of analytical review procedures and the nature of substitutes, rather than the nature or the timing of the procedures themselves. With this in mind, Chapter 6,

Using Analytical Review for Selected Accounts, will include a discussion of the relative efficiency of analytical review and tests of details for each account, in order to assist the auditor in choosing the extent to which analytical review should be used for each of the three engagement types. Chapter 7 is relevant only for the independent audit engagement since it relates to the use of analytical review in the final review. The other chapters deal only with the nature of analytical review procedures, so they are applicable for all three engagement types.

A FRAME OF REFERENCE FOR
ANALYTICAL REVIEW

In order to benefit fully from the book, it is important to have a frame of reference for organizing one's thinking about what analytical review consists of, and what knowledge, experience, information gathering, and information analysis are necessary to use it properly. The frame of reference we use is the distinction between two general methods for analytical review (see Table 1-1). Each of the two methods is a broad category encompassing steps and procedures which produce audit evidence through analysis of relationships between financial and operating data. Together, the methods include virtually all the steps and procedures which have been referred to as analytical review. Recognizing that auditors disagree about what should be labeled analytical review, our two methods are defined to be very comprehensive. The importance of the distinction between these methods is that they require a somewhat different nature and extent of auditor knowledge and experience. Also, the two methods have somewhat different demands for information gathering, evaluation, and analysis.

The two methods are:

1. *Risk analysis* requires the use of extensive accounting and business knowledge and experience to assess the potential for material misstatement in the financial statements taken as a whole. Often, this involves the analysis of financial ratios and indicators or the search for what has been called a "red flag," such as a turnover in key personnel, certain aspects of the audit history, or a change in credit rating. Risk analysis is covered in Chapters 2 and 7.

2. *Analytical review procedures* involve the use of a quantitative procedure to analyze the potential for misstatement in a single account, item, or element of the financial statements. Trend analysis, ratio analysis, and reasonableness tests are the common examples of analytical review

Table 1-1   Two Principal Analytical Review Methods

Characteristics of the Two Methods	Risk Analysis	Analytical Review Procedures
Primary objective	Analyze the potential for material misstatement in the financial statements taken as a whole.	Analyze the potential for material misstatement of a single financial statement account.
Procedure	Search for a "red flag," for example, turnover of key personnel, that often indicates the potential for material misstatement. Performed by management-level auditor.	Apply one or more of the three computational procedures: (1) trend analysis, (2) ratio analysis, or (3) reasonableness testing. Performed by auditor at the staff-in-charge level.
Required knowledge	A substantial knowledge about (1) the client's organization and business and (2) the financial and operating relationships of the client.	A good working knowledge of (1) the client's organization and business and (2) the financial and operating relationships of the client.
Required information	(1) Client financial and operating data and (2) other client data: correspondence, minutes of meetings, and so on.	Client financial and operating data.
Required evaluation and analysis	Typically negligible.	(1) Simple, though sometimes voluminous, calculations and (2) development of a prediction of what the account balance should be; comparison of this prediction to the reported amount; and analysis of the difference.

procedures. Ratio analysis is any method which involves comparing relationships between financial statement accounts (such as an expense-account-to-total-sales percentage), recognizing that the analysis of ratios often involves also considering the trend for the ratio. Trend analysis is the analysis of the change of an account balance over time. A reasonableness test is any computation used to estimate an account balance. Reasonableness tests usually require nonfinancial data. Analytical review procedures are covered in Chapters 3 through 6.

What knowledge, experience, and information are necessary to use each of these methods properly? For risk analysis to be effective, it is crucial that the auditor have extensive accounting and business knowledge and experience, since the key aspect of the task is to identify the relevant risk indicators and to interpret them properly. Thus, the analysis and evaluation of data per se is not an important feature of this method. In contrast, analytical review procedures often involve extensive data gathering and analysis and evaluation, as are required, for example, in the trend analysis of the working trial balance accounts. The key aspect of the task is to be able to consistently and correctly apply the procedure and to have the knowledge to interpret the procedure's results properly. Extensive accounting and business knowledge and experience are not as crucial a feature of this method, since the procedures are generally well known and easily understood. In summary, risk analysis can be characterized as an approach which tends to be somewhat open-ended and unstructured, and the judgments required are subjective in nature. On the other hand, analytical review procedures tend to be more well-defined and structured, and the judgments involved are more objective than is the case for risk analysis.

This frame of reference dictates the approach we take in the book. For example, the objective for the presentation of risk analysis in Chapters 2 and 7 is to describe a comprehensive set of techniques which the auditor can use to assess risk effectively. However, the auditor must use the judgment obtained from knowledge and experience to select and interpret these techniques properly in practice. In contrast, since analytical review procedures are more easily understood, the objective for the presentation in Chapters 3 through 6 is to explain methods for facilitating the use of the procedures (computer aids, etc.) and to describe the pitfalls that exist in applying and interpreting the procedures effectively. These chapters will also include suggestions for providing training and supervision of audit staff that will improve usage of analytical review.

HOW MUCH CAN THE AUDITOR RELY ON ANALYTICAL REVIEW?

To evaluate the strength of the evidence from analytical review, we must consider that analytical review provides a negative-type assurance rather than a positive one. That is, though analytical review can be a useful technique for detecting a material misstatement, it cannot be relied upon to confirm with positive assurance that a misstatement is *not* present.[1] Positive assurance comes only from the proper application of the appropriate detail test procedures. Thus, the auditor can never rely exclusively on analytical review when risk or materiality is high. But, the auditor does obtain reasonable assurance from analytical review by making the following four evaluations:

1. The auditor must be satisfied that the analytical review procedure is sufficiently *accurate*. That is, the analytical review must predict the account balance or relationship with good precision. The accuracy of an analytical review procedure is influenced both by the precision of the procedure and by the predictability of the underlying balance or relationship. For example, a statistical prediction (say, using regression) will generally be more precise than a nonstatistical prediction. Also, such account balances as depreciation expense, payroll expense, and interest expense are generally more easily predicted than accounts receivable or inventory. The auditor uses judgment to assess the precision of each analytical review application.

2. The auditor must also evaluate both the materiality and the risk of the account. *Materiality* relates to the potential significance of misstatements in the account, and *risk* relates to the potential that an error occurs and is not detected by the entity's controls. The auditor can obtain reasonable assurance from analytical review if both risk and materiality are low.

3. Since the risk of an account is influenced by the quality of the entity's accounting controls, the auditor's reliance on analytical review is directly related to the evaluation of *controls*. If the proper controls are in place and are complied with, the auditor can obtain more assurance from the analytical review.

4. The nature and effectiveness of *other audit procedures* also influences the auditor's reliance on analytical review. If other procedures are effective, and these procedures uncover no significant errors or irregularities, then the analytical review can provide reasonable assurance.

Auditor Mistakes and Risks

When considering the degree of reliance to be placed on analytical review, it is helpful to understand the types of mistakes the auditor can make, and the related risks. There are two types of mistakes the auditor can make using analytical review:

Type 1: The results of an analytical review indicate to the auditor that a material misstatement is present, when it is not.

Type 2: The results of an analytical review indicate to the auditor that a material misstatement is *not* present, when in fact it is.

The cost of the type 1 mistake is the unnecessary additional auditing undertaken by the auditor. The type 2 mistake has no immediate cost, but subjects the auditor to the risk of significant later costs if the auditor gives a clean report and the material misstatement is subsequently detected. A high rate of type 1 mistakes can be related to audit inefficiency, whereas a high rate of type 2 mistakes could be related to ineffectiveness. Avoiding the type 2 mistake is ordinarily the auditor's principal concern because of the potentially high cost of legal liability and related costs.

The chance that an auditor will make the type 2 mistake is called the "risk" of the type 2 mistake. Risk is a percentage or probability, between 0 and 1. The extent to which an analytical review procedure reduces this risk is a good measure of the usefulness of the procedure and the reliance the auditor can obtain from it.

When one is considering risk and reliance for analytical review, it is important to consider the full scope of audit procedures—internal control evaluation and testing, analytical review, and tests of details—and the risk that all the procedures will make the type 2 mistake in a given set of circumstances.[2] Audit risk is expressed as the simple product of the individual risk of the type 2 mistake for each of the three procedures. Thus

$$R = IR \times IC \times AR \times TD$$

where R = audit risk that a material misstatement is not detected

       IR = risk that a material misstatement occurs (the inherent risk)

       IC = risk that the material misstatement is not prevented or detected by the system of internal accounting controls

      AR = risk that the material misstatement is not detected by analytical review

      TD = risk that the material misstatement is not detected by tests of details

For example, if we make the conservative assumption that a material misstatement is present (i.e., $IR = 1.0$), and we assume that the risk of a type 2 mistake for each procedure is 20 percent (i.e., $IC = AR = TD = .2$), then audit risk can be calculated as the chance of 8 in 1000.

$$R = 1.0 \times .2 \times .2 \times .2 = .008$$

Audit risk is very small because each of the three procedures is assumed to act independently to detect the misstatement, so that the auditor obtains increased assurance, with each additional procedure, that no material misstatement is present. Since the auditor's overall concern is audit risk, rather than its three components, each of the three procedures can be viewed as "compensating" for the risk associated with the other two. Thus, a high risk of the type 2 mistake for internal controls (say, IC = .5) can be compensated by a lower risk for tests of details (say, TD = .08). Therefore

$$R = 1.0 \times .5 \times .2 \times .08 = .008$$

This latter example would reflect a case wherein the controls are weaker but the tests of details are stronger than for the original example.

In summary, since the risk associated with each of the three procedures affects audit risk, and since reduced risk for any one can offset increased risk for any other, the reliance the auditor can place on analytical review must be considered together with the evaluation of controls and the planned extent of tests of details. The stronger the other two procedures (low TD and IC), the less the needed reliance on analytical review (AR can be high) to achieve acceptable audit risk. Conversely, if the auditor judges the analytical review to be strong, then TD or IC can be proportionately higher. The auditor's judgments about the strength of an analytical review procedure and about the inversely related risk level are based on the timing, nature, and extent of the procedure. In general terms, the strength of a procedure is proportional to the accuracy, relevance, timeliness, and extensiveness of the data which are used to predict and analyze the account balance or relationship. Each of Chapters 2, 3, 4, and 5 will include a discussion of this judgment process as it applies to the analytical review procedure discussed in that chapter.

SUMMARY—STATE OF THE ART

This chapter has provided an introduction to analytical review and to the book. In summary, we now reflect on some of the findings of our research and of other researchers who have studied the practice of analytical review. A consideration of these findings will show why and how the book can assist you in using analytical review procedures.

The most striking finding of these studies is the lack of consensus among auditors regarding the role and effectiveness of analytical review procedures. Though some auditors see analytical review as an important planning tool, many others prefer using the results of the analytical review to corroborate other knowledge, rather than to serve as the initial source for audit planning decisions. In effect, they do not consider analytical review to be the independent and effective source of audit evidence we have assumed it to be in the previously presented formula for audit risk. Some of the reasons for this view have been expressed as follows:

1. When, as is often the case, the analytical review is based upon a comparison of financial data across time, a meaningful analysis is frequently not possible because the data are not comparable owing to significant changes in accounting methods, operating factors, and so on.
2. Certain analytical review procedures require operating data and other types of data which are outside the system of internal accounting controls; these data are not ordinarily processed with the same standards of accuracy as financial data are.
3. Many auditors feel that methods relating economic events to financial results are too imprecise, that is, that they often lead the auditor to a wrong conclusion. Further, statistical and other methods which improve this precision are not cost-beneficial.
4. Available auditing literature is inadequate in explaining in a useable fashion how analytical review procedures are applied and how to avoid judgment errors which are inherent in using the procedures.
5. Analytical review is not well-defined. This leads directly to a lack of consensus among auditors and a lack of consistency for each auditor when applying the procedures. This also leads indirectly to a communication problem between audit team members which conflicts which the effectiveness of the planning, supervision, and review of the engagement.
6. At this point, auditing lacks the important integrative concepts which would help to bring some focus and consensus to the thinking about analytical review. For example, the concepts of a "processing cycle" and of a "boundary" have had a key role in the development of improved methods for evaluating internal accounting controls.

While some of the above difficulties are not easily solved and thus represent a persistent limitation on the usefulness of analytical review, others relate only to a lack of understanding of how to use analytical review properly.

The book is intended to address this latter problem. Further, our approach proceeds from the belief that a single analytical review procedure which is low-cost, which is generally applicable, and which gives the necessary narrow precision is currently beyond our grasp. Rather, we present the auditor with a menu of easy-to-use procedures in a reference format.

FOOTNOTES

[1]However, one recent study has shown that a substantial proportion of errors are initially identified by analytical review procedures (Hylas and Ashton, 1982). This suggests that analytical review can be more effective than is generally recognized.

[2]Currently, it is common in the professional literature to refer to the risk associated with analytical review and tests of details as "detection risk." Detection risk then is the combined risk for both types of substantive test procedures. We distinguish the two risks (AR and TD) in our discussion to highlight the role of analytical review and the risk associated with it.

REFERENCES

Hylas, Robert E., and Robert H. Ashton: "Audit Detection of Financial Statement Errors," *Accounting Review,* October 1982, pp. 751–765.

chapter
two

Analyzing and Evaluating Inherent Risk

The analysis and evaluation of inherent risk are central to the auditor's development of the scope and plan for an audit engagement. *Inherent risk* is the chance that a material error will occur. Management reduces this risk by employing a sound system of internal accounting controls, and the auditor reduces the risk further by evaluation and testing of the controls and through tests of account balances. The combined risk that the error will occur and not be detected either by the management control system or by the auditor is the audit risk.

Inherent risk is commonly analyzed and evaluated during the planning phase. The analysis has two aspects: (1) the use of selected nonquantitative procedures, which we have described as "risk analysis," and (2) the use of well-known analytical review procedures, such as trend analysis and ratio analysis. The elements of risk analysis include assessments of management integrity, an evaluation of the entity's going-concern status, and the like. Trend analysis at this point would focus on the trend in earnings, in selected liquidity measures, and in cash flow. The ratio analysis would be employed to evaluate the entity's liquidity and profitability position relative to other firms in the industry and to the firm's position in prior years. Since there is ordinarily some variability among firms regarding liquidity and profitability, the analysis of these ratios over time is often given priority over the intra-industry comparison.

Upon completion of these analyses, the auditor combines the results to obtain an overall evaluation of inherent risk. This evaluation is the basis for choosing the required scope of audit field work—with greater scope for higher risk. Figure 2-1 summarizes this discussion, to show how the audit risk, the phases of the audit engagement, and the two analytical review methods are related in the analysis of inherent risk.

THREE ASPECTS OF INHERENT RISK

Inherent risk has three readily distinguishable aspects which can be analyzed separately. Each aspect is a type of risk, and each is influenced by different factors in the entity's environment. The existence of any of these three risks signals a potential motivation or opportunity on the part of the entity's management or personnel to introduce a material misstatement to the accounting records, whether intentionally or not. And the greater the risk for any of the three, the greater is inherent risk. The common terms for these three risks are operating risk, financial risk, and market risk.[1] Note that each of the three aspects of inherent risk differs in nature from the concept of "business risk," a term which has been used to refer to the risk of loss or injury to the CPA's professional practice, apart from whether or not an undetected material misstatement is present. However, many of the factors which influence inherent risk are among the factors which also influence business risk, so there is some commonality for these risk concepts. We feel the best way to achieve an understanding of the role of analytical review in auditing is to consider the three aspects of inherent risk defined above.

Operating risk is associated with the chance that earnings or liquidity position or both will fluctuate unacceptably for reasons related to the nature of the entity's business environment—seasonal or otherwise high-risk products and services, severe competition, general economic condi-

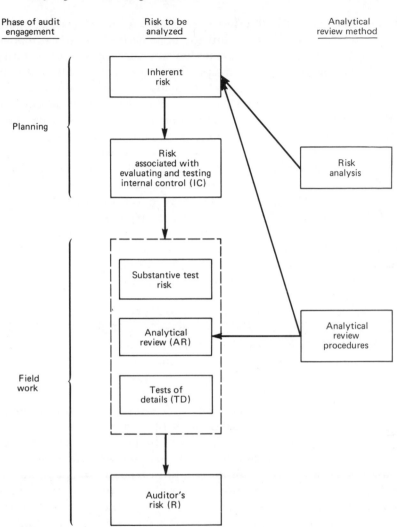

Figure 2-1 Inherent risk, audit risk, analytical review, and the phases of the audit engagement.

tions affecting the industry, and the like. Many of these factors are not easily controlled by management in the short term; rather, they are managed through diversification and careful long-range planning. To the extent that these factors threaten the going-concern position of the entity, by eroding earnings or liquidity, risk of material misstatement of the financial statements increases, as does inherent risk.

Financial risk is associated with the entity's ability to meet debt commitments. Because of a desire to achieve a high degree of financial leverage, or because of an inability to obtain acceptable equity financing, a firm might accumulate a high proportion of debt to equity and high interest charges relative to earnings from operations. The amount of debt relative to equity, the portion of debt which is short-term, the nature of credit relationships generally, and the strength of cash flows from operations will together determine whether the firm has significant financial risk. Again, to the extent the going-concern position of the entity is threatened, financial risk and inherent risk are increased.

Market risk is associated with the variability of the entity's stock prices. Significant fluctuations in an entity's stock price relative to the overall stock market would reflect investors' perceptions that the future returns from the stock are relatively risky. In contrast, stocks with relatively stable prices are associated with relatively lower market risk. Market risk can also be affected by significant changes in stock ownership, by significant inside trading and proxy fights, and the like. Some would say that a high price-to-earnings ratio is an additional sign of relatively high market risk.

Market risk influences inherent risk because it is important in shareholder perceptions of the entity, and thereby can influence management behavior. However, it is not usually associated with the assessment of the going-concern position of the entity, as are operating and financial risk. For this reason it has a lesser impact on inherent risk, and is of lesser concern to the auditor.

On reflection, it is clear that these three risks are not strictly independent. That is, both operating risk and financial risk should influence investors' risk perceptions and thereby influence market risk. Thus, the three risks do not simply "add together" to determine inherent risk, and the auditor's overall evaluation of risk must take this into account. Also, the overall evaluation of inherent risk must include the auditor's assessment of management integrity, apart from the analysis of the three risk factors. That is, a high positive assessment of management integrity could alleviate an otherwise high evaluation of inherent risk. The assessment of management integrity could include an evaluation of ethical standards, the degree of conservatism in income-recognition policy and other accounting matters, and management's openness with internal and external auditors.

The three risk factors and the evaluation of management integrity are combined to obtain the initial assessment of inherent risk. This risk is reduced by management through two levels of controls: (1) controls which simultaneously reduce the risk of misstatement for many or all financial statement accounts, items, or elements and (2) controls which reduce risk for a single account, item, or element. We refer to the former as "organizational controls" and to the latter as "internal accounting controls."[2] We make this distinction to facilitate our discussion of inherent risk. Because of the diversity of types of internal accounting controls for different purposes, we do not attempt to develop in this book an approach for evaluating these controls, and for assessing the extent to which they reduce inherent risk. On the other hand, the review of organizational controls involves a relatively well-defined set of key variables which are common for most organizations. For this reason, the chapter deals with organizational controls only. Additionally, our interest is in analytical review, and the review of organizational controls is often considered an analytical review since it is directed to developing an understanding of the entity's business and organization. The relationships between the factors influencing inherent risk are summarized in Figure 2-2.

The following four sections of the chapter will develop a framework for the auditor's use in analyzing operating risk, financial risk, management integrity, and organizational controls, each of which has a major influence on inherent risk. Market risk is not included because it has a relatively less important influence on inherent risk. The chapter concludes with a discussion of methods for aggregating the auditor's evaluation of the three risk types, the organizational controls, and the integrity of management, in order to obtain an overall evaluation of inherent risk.

ANALYZING OPERATING RISK

The objective of the auditor's analysis of operating risk is to identify and evaluate those operational characteristics of the auditee's business and organization which contribute to inherent risk. These characteristics may contribute to risk in either of two ways: (1) by motivating the auditee's management or employees to cause and not disclose a misstatement of the accounts or (2) by making it more difficult for management to prevent or detect any misstatement, apart from the effectiveness of the control system employed. The characteristics in the first case are often those related to the financial performance and position of the auditee, or to the financial need of an employee, while the characteristics in the second case are most often related to the complexity of the organization—diversity and turnover of product lines, decentralization, geographic dispersion, and so on.

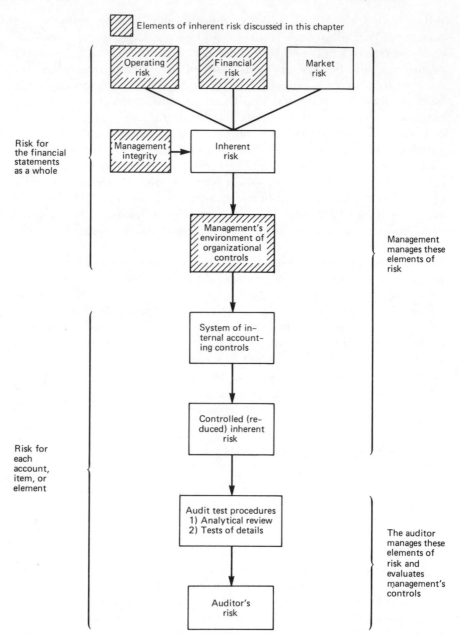

Figure 2-2   Inherent risk and related factors.

The auditor should look for these characteristics in at least five areas, each of which could provide the motivation, opportunity, or both for misstatement:

1. Sales
2. Production and distribution
3. Organizational structure
4. Legal or regulatory matters
5. Other restrictive commitments

A useful approach for this analysis is to use a checklist in the format of the questionnaire that is often used in audit planning, review, and internal control evaluation. The questionnaire would list the relevant characteristics in each of the five areas, and the auditor would indicate the presence and severity of the risk for each characteristic.

Sales

In analyzing the auditee's sales the auditor is looking primarily for indications of substantial current or near-term deterioration in sales performance. First, the auditor should consider the characteristics of the industry environment in which the auditee firm operates. Does the firm operate in a local, regional, or international market? How do recent and pending governmental regulations and trade agreements, if any, affect the industry? The auditor can find answers to these and related questions through:

1. Advice from industry specialists within the auditor's firm
2. Trade association publications
3. Consultants and economists specializing in the industry
4. Banks and insurance agents who specialize in servicing the industry

From such sources the auditor can determine if there is a significant potential change in sales trend for the industry.

A second level of questions would address the auditee firm's effectiveness in developing a marketing plan. Does the firm analyze its market share in sufficient detail to detect significant regional and local shifts? Are sales forecasts made, and, if so, how are they obtained? How accurate are they? Has management developed an appropriate plan for product diversification? Is there a competitive strategy; that is, has the firm chosen to compete on price, quality, service, or some other factor, and how well has this positioned it in the market? The study of these questions will help the auditor assess the strength of sales performance in coming months.

On a third level, the auditor looks for certain external factors affecting the competitive environment of the firm. Has the firm experienced recent unfavorable publicity because of questions of product quality, safety, or other matters? Has there recently been a substantial shift in marketing strategy in response to competition? In particular, has advertising become more defensive in nature? Do the firm's competitors appear to be gaining a technological edge in product quality, performance, or cost?

On the positive side, the auditor should also take note of a substantial growth in sales. If the growth outstrips management's span of control, the chance of unintentional misstatement is increased until the accounting system is upgraded. Also, a significant growth in sales that is not explained directly by industry and market conditions should be investigated, especially if management compensation is strongly influenced by sales.

Production and Distribution

As with sales, the auditor studies the firm's production and distribution system in order to detect whether any factors have, or could have in the near term, a damaging effect on the firm's operations. For example, is the availability of necessary materials at reasonable prices assured? Is a change in plant location planned? What is the status of labor relations, and when does the current contract expire? Will a new production process be implemented in the near term? If so, what will be the extent of disruption? Analysis of these questions will enable the auditor to assess the potential for risk associated with production. Similar questions should be asked for the firm's distribution system.

Organizational Structure

Because of their complexity, some organizational structures are inherently more risky than others. For example, firms which grow by internal expansion of facilities, personnel, and management are inherently less risky than those which grow by merger and acquisition. The latter face difficulties of maintaining standards of quality control and maintaining continuity of management policy; they lack goal congruity and consistency in accounting and internal reporting systems, and have related problems. Also, expansion of any type exposes the firm to risks when the new markets are not well understood by management, particularly new international markets. The auditor must assess the risk associated with the expansion by evaluating management's ability to control the incremental activity of expansion, giving special attention to the method of expansion and geographical dispersion.

A second and related issue for organizational structure is the extent of product diversification. As above, the greater the diversification, the greater will be the demand on management's ability to control operations. Does management have the necessary expertise to control and evaluate operations in each line of business? Has management developed a uniform accounting and internal reporting system for all segments? The latter is particularly important because of management's line-of-business reporting responsibility to the Securities and Exchange Commission (SEC), and because of the auditor's related auditing requirements.

The above issues are aggravated by the autonomy of segment managers, which is typically associated with the extensively diversified firm. Also, the accounting for discontinued operations, associated with these firms, contributes to inherent risk because of the unique nature of the accounting transactions.

Legal or Regulatory Matters

In some cases, legal or regulatory matters may represent a significant risk to operations. License, patent, or copyright litigation is one example. Also, pending legislation at the state or federal level could have a substantial impact on competition in the firm's industry. Or, the firm itself may be involved in important litigation with a customer or competitor, the results of which could seriously impact its ability to compete in the industry. The auditor investigates these matters by consulting industry experts, the firm's legal counsel, and the SEC to determine the nature and extent of any pending litigation, regulation, or inquiries. Also, the auditor should stay informed of the progress of relevant state or federal legislation through reference to trade or industry publications and consultants.

Other Restrictive Commitments

Various trade and labor commitments can affect the firm's risk of operations by reducing its flexibility in dealing with competitive pressures within the industry. The auditor should check especially for restrictive commitments in the following areas: (1) lease contracts for facilities or major equipment, (2) labor contracts, and (3) marketing agreements. The best source of this information is usually inquiry of the firm's management, labor union management, and industry consultants.

Evaluating Operating Risk

The above discussion provides a basis for the auditor to uncover several possible indicators of operating risk. To come up with an aggregate

Publication	Publisher
Dun's	Dun's Review 666 Fifth Avenue New York, NY 10019
Sources of Composite Financial Data and Annual Statement Studies	Robert Morris Associates Philadelphia National Bank Building Philadelphia, PA 19107
Quarterly Financial Report for Manufacturing Corporations *Survey of Current Business*	Superintendent of Documents U.S. Government Printing Office Washington, DC 20402
Almanac of Business and Industrial Financial Ratios, by Leo Troy	Prentice-Hall, Inc. Englewood Cliffs, NJ 07632
Compustat Industry Data	Standard and Poor's Compustat Services, Inc. 345 Hudson Street New York, NY 10014

evaluation, the auditor should consider whether any of the indicators observed as "negative" (i.e., risky), taken individually, or together with other negative indicators, is so substantial as to require adjustment to the scope of planned audit tests. Additionally, the auditor should prepare an analysis of selected financial ratios for the most current 3 years, as a basis for assessing the trend in these indicators of operating risk. The four ratios most commonly used in evaluating profitability are:

1. Earnings per share
2. Return on assets
3. Return on equity
4. Net profit to sales

A significant deterioration in any of these ratios over the 3-year period would signal increased operating risk. Also, the firm's ratios should be compared with industry statistics relevant for its line of business. Again, significant differences are a signal of operating risk. However, since industry averages are often inappropriate benchmarks for a given firm, because of unique factors affecting the firm, the auditor should place principal reliance on the trend in the ratios and use the industry comparison secondarily.[3] A condensed list of sources of industry statistics is given in the table shown above. For a longer list of sources that offer industry statistics, see Exhibit 3 at the end of Chapter 4.

ANALYZING FINANCIAL RISK

The auditor analyzes the financial structure of the firm to assess the inherent risk associated with its ability to meet debt commitments, primarily short-term debt commitments but also ones in the long term. Hereafter, we will refer to the ability to meet short-term debt as "liquidity" and the ability to meet long-term obligations as "leverage."

The auditor should consider two methods of analysis for financial risk. One method looks at the going-concern question; that is, do we predict the firm will become bankrupt within our planning period? This can be viewed as the extreme or ultimate measure of financial risk and, as such, will be appropriate only in rare instances. The second method of analysis looks at the less severe conditions, which we call "financial distress." This means the firm is in a position which could lead to failure, if not corrected. We assume the means for correction are at hand, however. Each form of analysis is addressed in the following discussion.

Predicting Bankruptcy

The auditor can use either a "key indicator" or a "fundamental analysis" approach to predict bankruptcy. The indicator-based approach is useful for determining whether the firm is at or very near the bankruptcy state, whereas fundamental analysis can provide a meaningful prediction for 2 to 5 years into the future. The fundamental analysis approach is generally less accurate but is more useful since it can predict for a longer period.

Some of the key indicators used by auditors are listed below. The appearance of one or more of these indicators would signal the potential of imminent bankruptcy.

1. Current liabilities greater than current assets
2. Default in loan payment
3. Renegotiation of lease or other debt
4. Projected cash flow from operations which is less than the amount of maturing debt
5. Total liabilities greater than total assets

The auditor should carefully consider the substance behind these indicators. That is, the company may attempt to renegotiate a lease for a good business purpose such as to obtain a lower-cost lease. In this case the event does not indicate pending bankruptcy.

The fundamental analysis approach is based primarily upon the analysis of financial ratios.[4] The two prominent studies of ratios used for bankruptcy prediction are those by Beaver (1966) and Altman (1968).

Table 2-1   Ratios Used to Predict Bankruptcy*

Type of Ratio	Beaver's Ratio	Altman's Ratios
Operating ratios	Return on total assets (2)	Return on total assets (1) Sales to total assets (2)
Leverage ratios	Total debt to total assets (3) Cash flow to total debt (1)†	Market value of equity to total debt (3)
Liquidity ratios	Working capital to total assets (4) Current ratio (5)	Working capital to total assets (5)
Other predictors	(Quick assets − current liabilities) to operating expenses (excluding depreciation)	Retained earnings to total assets (4)

*Adapted from studies by Beaver (1966) and Altman (1968). The ranking of the relative importance of each ratio in each of the studies is indicated in parentheses after each ratio.

†Beaver found this ratio to be the most useful in discriminating between bankrupt and nonbankrupt firms. However, Altman was unable to use a cash flow variable since he did not have depreciation figures and could not compute cash flow, so we cannot know whether this variable would have performed equally well for Altman.

The ratios found to be most predictive of bankruptcy are shown in Table 2-1. These studies applied a statistical methodology to determine the most predictive set of ratios, so the ratios can be viewed as the key variables in identifying potential bankruptcy cases. Note that the results of the two studies are consistent. Operating and leverage ratios are most important, while liquidity ratios are not good predictors. Auditors should consider the significance of this evidence, in part because the conventional wisdom says that the current ratio, the turnover ratios (receivables, inventory), and other liquidity measures are key variables in analyzing financial risk. These results suggest that other ratios are better predictors.

Our classification of ratios—operating, leverage, and liquidity ratios—is among the most commonly used in financial statement analysis textbooks. Table 2-2 shows the 24 most important ratios and how they are computed.

A useful aspect of the Altman model is that it permits the computation of a numerical ranking of the bankruptcy potential of a firm. It is called the Altman Z-score and is computed as follows

$$Z\text{-score} = 3.3(\text{return on total assets})$$
$$+ 0.99(\text{sales to total assets})$$
$$+ 0.6(\text{market value of equity to total debt})$$
$$+ 1.2(\text{working capital to total assets})$$
$$+ 1.4(\text{retained earnings to total assets})$$

Table 2-2 Important Ratios and How They Are Computed

Operating ratios

1. Return on sales

$$\frac{\text{Profits before tax and extraordinary items}}{\text{Net sales}}$$

2. Return on total assets

$$\frac{\text{Profits before tax and extraordinary items} + \text{interest}}{\text{Average total assets}}$$

3. Return on tangible net worth

$$\frac{\text{Profits before tax and extraordinary items}}{\text{Average tangible net worth}^a}$$

4. Percentage profit change

$$\frac{\begin{array}{l}\text{Current year's profit} \\ \text{before tax and} \\ \text{extraordinary items}\end{array} - \begin{array}{l}\text{last year's profit} \\ \text{before tax and} \\ \text{extraordinary items}\end{array}}{\text{Last year's profit before tax and extraordinary items}}$$

5. Percentage sales change

$$\frac{\text{Current year's sales} - \text{last year's sales}}{\text{Last year's sales}}$$

6. Sales to total assets

$$\frac{\text{Sales}}{\text{Total assets}}$$

7. Coefficient of variation of net income

$$\frac{\text{Standard deviation of net income}}{\text{Average net income}}$$

Leverage ratios

8. Long-term debt to capitalization

$$\frac{\text{Long-term debt}^b}{\text{Long-term debt} + \text{stockholders' equity}}$$

9. Net tangible assets to long-term debt

$$\frac{\text{Net tangible assets}^c}{\text{Long-term debt}}$$

10. Working capital to long-term debt

$$\frac{\text{Working capital}^d}{\text{Long-term debt}}$$

11. Fixed-charge coverage

$$\frac{\text{Aftertax net income} + \text{interest} + \text{rentals}}{\text{Interest} + \text{rentals}}$$

12. Cash flow to total debt

$$\frac{\text{Cash flow}^e}{\text{Total debt}}$$

13. Total debt to total assets

$$\frac{\text{Total debt}}{\text{Total assets}}$$

14. Market value of equity to book value of debt

$$\frac{\text{Market value of equity}}{\text{Total debt}}$$

15. Interest coverage

$$\frac{\text{Aftertax net income} + \text{interest}}{\text{Interest}}$$

16. Long-term debt to equity

$$\frac{\text{Long-term debt}}{\text{Stockholders' equity}}$$

17. Tangible net worth to total debt

$$\frac{\text{Average tangible net worth}}{\text{Total debt}}$$

Table 2-2 Important Ratios and How They Are Computed (*Continued*)

Liquidity ratios

18. Working capital to total assets

$$\dfrac{\text{Working capital}}{\text{Total assets}}$$

19. Current ratio

$$\dfrac{\text{Current assets}}{\text{Current liabilities}}$$

20. Quick (acid-test) ratio

$$\dfrac{\text{Cash} + \text{marketable securities} + \text{net current receivables}}{\text{Current liabilities}}$$

21. Liquidity ratio

$$\dfrac{\text{Cash} + \text{marketable securities} + \text{net current receivables}}{\text{Short-term debt}^{f}}$$

22. Working capital turnover

$$\dfrac{\text{Sales}}{\text{Average working capital}}$$

23. Accounts receivable turnover

$$\dfrac{\text{Net sales}}{\text{Average receivables}}$$

24. Inventory turnover

$$\dfrac{\text{Cost of goods sold}}{\text{Average inventory}}$$

---

*a*Tangible net worth = stockholders' equity − intangible assets.

*b*Long-term debt = long-term liabilities − (deferred taxes + minority interest).

*c*Net tangible assets = total assets − (intangible assets + current liabilities + deferred taxes + minority interest).

*d*Working capital = current assets − current liabilities.

*e*Cash flow = aftertax net income − extraordinary items + depreciation and amortization + deferred taxes.

*f*Short-term debt = notes due within 1 year + current portion of long-term debt.

SOURCE: Adapted from Backer and Gosman (1978), pp. 119–120.

The lower the Z-score, the greater the chance of bankruptcy. If the Z-score is less than 1.81, there is a strong potential for bankruptcy within the next 2 years, whereas a Z-score above 2.99 indicates little chance for bankruptcy. In the range between 1.81 and 2.99 there is an increased chance for incorrectly classifying a firm. In computing and interpreting the Z-score, the auditor should be aware that:

1. The Z-score is not accurate beyond 2 years into the future; it is most accurate for a 1-year prediction, least accurate for a 2-year prediction.[5] The 2-year model is very conservative; it tends to predict bankruptcy for firms which remain going concerns. Altman and McGough (1974) review the empirical evidence for the model.

2. Three of the ratios—return on total assets, working capital to total assets, and retained earnings to total assets—can be negative, and therefore will be subtracted in obtaining the Z-score.

3. The ratios are entered into the model as decimals rather than absolute percentage terms (for example, sales/assets = 2.0, rather than 200.0 percent).

4. The model assumes that the underlying financial data are reliable.

5. The model applies to manufacturing firms only.

Predicting Financial Distress

Financial distress is a less severe condition than bankruptcy, but it contributes to inherent risk by creating an environment in which management is motivated to misstate certain financial data. This condition exists when the financing options are limited owing to a downgrading of bonds, deterioration of cash flows, and so on.

As for bankruptcy, the auditor's analysis of financial distress can take either a key indicator or a fundamental analysis approach. One or more of the key indicators in the following list would signal current or near-term financial distress. The first indicator, cash flow, is especially important.

1. Unfavorable trend in cash flows.

2. A low current bond or trade credit rating.

3. A recent downgrade of bond rating or trade credit rating.

4. A bank classification of a loan as substandard.

5. Imminent violation of loan agreement restrictions on cash flow, liquidity, etc.

6. Disruption in relationships with bankers and brokers.

7. Past-due payables or extensions of payment terms. (Note, however, that because suppliers are the least likely to complain about delay of payment, this indicator may not be easily obtained.)

By the nature of the markets for these instruments, a downgrading of bonds should be an earlier signal of financial distress than the downgrading of trade credit. Similarly, the downgrading of trade credit should occur before a loan is rated substandard by a bank.

Fundamental analysis has been used to study the relationship between the downgrading of bonds and financial ratios. The results of these studies are shown in Table 2-3. Notice again that operating and leverage ratios are consistently the best predictors of bond downgrading. Liquidity ratios are rarely used. The auditor should then interpret a significant unfavorable trend in any of these ratios as a signal of potential financial

Table 2-3 Ratios Used to Predict the Downgrading of Bond Ratings

Type of Ratio	Researchers				
	Horrigan	Pogue and Soldofsky	West	Pinches and Mingo	Backer and Gosman
Operating ratios	Return on sales Return on tangible net worth	Return on total assets Coefficient of variation of net income	Coefficient of variation of net income	Return on total assets	Return on sales Return on total assets
Leverage ratios	Tangible net worth to total debt	Long-term debt to capitalization Interest coverage	Long-term debt to equity	Long-term debt to total assets Interest coverage	Long-term debt to capitalization Cash flow to long-term debt
Liquidity ratios	Working capital turnover	None	None	None	None
Other predictors	Subordination status of bonds Total assets	Total assets	Market value of bonds	Subordination status of bonds Years of consecutive dividends Issue size	None

SOURCES: Adapted from Horrigan (1966), Pogue and Soldofsky (1969), West (1970), Pinches and Mingo (1973), and Backer and Gosman (1978).

distress. The ratios used specifically in financial institutions, utilities, and the transportation industry are shown in Table 2-4.

Another source for predicting the downgrading of bonds is Standard and Poor's *Credit Watch,* which lists firms whose rating status is currently under review.

Suggestions for Using Fundamental Analysis

The proper use of fundamental analysis based on financial ratios will be facilitated by attention to the following matters:[6]

1. Ratios should be compared primarily over time, and secondarily to industry benchmarks, for the reasons already cited. Often, there are reasons why a firm's ratios differ from industry standards which do not reflect financial risk.

With further analysis, however, the auditor can obtain useful additional information by comparing the trend of the firm's ratios with the trend of the ratios for the industry group. *Industrial Compustat,* a service of Standard and Poor's Inc., provides aggregate industry data at useful levels of detail to facilitate an analysis of this type. To obtain the analysis in a timely and cost-effective manner, the auditor would maintain the *Compustat* data on computer and develop computer programs to compute and present the desired ratios in an easy-to-use fashion. For example, with proper programming the auditor-user would be able to input the firm's data code number into the computer and receive promptly a preselected analysis of the firm's ratios and the related industry ratios. The ratios could be presented in a columnar format to facilitate the auditor's comparison of firm versus industry trends.

Table 2-4   Financial Distress Ratios for Certain Industries

	Financial Institutions	Utilities	Transportation
Operating ratios	Operating expenses to operating revenue	Operating revenue to operating property Operating expense to operating revenue	Operating expense to operating revenue
Leverage ratios	Capital funds to total assets Total deposits to capital	Funded debt to operating property Interest coverage	Long-term debt to operating property
Liquidity ratios	Loans to total deposits		

The data available on *Compustat* include approximately 2000 companies and 100 industry categories for both quarterly (40 periods) or annual (20 years) data. The data are continually updated; thus, they are timely enough for most audit planning purposes.

2. There is no evidence that any predetermined level for any ratio can be used as a benchmark for assessing financial risk. As above, differences in ratios may not reflect differences in risk. For example, whether the firm is a very new and growing entity and whether it is closely held are among the factors which should affect the interpretation of the ratio. Also, Backer and Gosman (1978, p. 18) found no evidence of the use of ratio benchmarks in their study of bond and trade credit rating decisions. Thus, the use of a single ratio benchmark does not appear to be appropriate. As noted above, it is the *trend* of the ratio relative to the industry *trend* which is useful, rather than the comparison of ratios for 1 year only.

3. Largay and Stickney (1980) in a study of the W. T. Grant Company failure show that ratio analyses did not provide an early signal of bankruptcy, whereas a cash flow analysis would have given an early signal. The ratios did not deteriorate significantly up to the date of failure, while the amount of cash flow generated internally declined steeply for 5 to 6 years before the bankruptcy. This illustrates that ratio analysis by itself is an incomplete fundamental analysis and should be extended by analysis of cash flows, the firm's competitive environment, critical macroeconomic factors for the firm, and so on.

4. The problem of comparability is enlarged by the variety of accounting conventions which may change within the firm over time. The auditor should watch for consistent treatment of the following:

    a. Leases—included in long-term debt?
    b. Minority interest—an element of total capital?
    c. Subordinated debt—debt or equity?
    d. Pension reserves—debt or equity?
    e. Deferred taxes—debt, capital, or asset offset?
    f. Intangibles—deleted?

5. The use of ratios is subject to the same limitations as for the underlying financial data, for example:

    a. Lack of data in constant dollars or current dollars
    b. Effect of accounting estimates
    c. Effect of management discretion on inventory levels and unit costs
    d. Effect of officers' salaries in closely held companies

6. The untrained auditor may assume incorrectly that, since ratios are numbers, there is a simple linear significance to them; that is, a current ratio of 1.5 is perceived to be "twice as bad" as a ratio of 3.0, when in fact it is many times worse. This is particularly important, for example, when a given ratio approaches the limit set in a loan covenant. If the firm must maintain a current ratio of 2.0 or better, then a deterioration from 2.0 to 1.9 is much more severe than a deterioration from 3.0 to 2.85, though both represent a 5 percent decline.

7. Fundamental analysis may be available through purchase from industry specialists or financial analysts. These analyses are produced on a timely basis for stock exchange—listed companies and other large companies.

Evaluating Financial Risk

The auditor's evaluation of financial risk is based upon a review of the distress indicators and of the trend of the financial ratios noted above. If one or more of the indicators or ratios indicate a deterioration of financial position and higher risk, the auditor will consider the significance for audit scope and coverage. In making this evaluation, the auditor should recognize the special importance of evaluating the amount, timing, and certainty of expected cash inflows and outflows. This is one of the most critical factors in financial risk.

It may help the auditor, in making this evaluation, to consider how flexible the firm is in financial matters. How quickly could the firm reduce costs if necessary? Could certain maintenance costs or research and development costs be delayed without serious long-run effects? And, how flexible is the firm's dividend policy? Could dividends be reduced without serious effects? Also, does the firm have a favorable relationship with creditors which would make ready access to short-term loans possible? And finally, could the firm dispose of certain assets for a substantial return, without significantly affecting its ability to operate? Consideration of these questions could provide additional insight into the evaluation of financial risk.

ANALYZING MANAGEMENT INTEGRITY

Apart from the motivation for misstatement contributed by operating or financial risk, the auditor should evaluate management's propensity to respond with openness and integrity. Does management show a tendency for earnings maximization and manipulation by various means? The auditor will ordinarily have a sense of this from working with the firm's management in planning the audit. Indicators of potential problems include:

1. A decision to change to deferral of items ordinarily expensed
2. A tendency to make transactions or accruals of questionable economic substance
3. Economic trouble in other matters on the part of managers or owners
4. A change in discount policy for unsalable inventory
5. A change in credit policy for uncollectible accounts receivable

Indicators such as the above should heighten the auditor's awareness of the potential effect on inherent risk. For a more complete study of management fraud, see Albrecht et al. (1982) and Elliott and Willingham (1980).

ANALYZING ORGANIZATIONAL CONTROLS

Organizational controls are the administrative policies and procedures designed to reduce the chance for a material misstatement in any aspect of the financial statements.[7]

Firm Characteristics Which Make Control Difficult

Before reviewing the elements of a sound system of organizational controls, we consider the characteristics of the firm which generally make controls difficult to implement effectively:[8]

1. Decentralization of any of the functions—production, marketing, finance, controllership
2. Geographic dispersion
3. Rapid growth of the firm or the industry
4. Recent growth by acquisition rather than internal expansion
5. Unsupportive attitude of top management toward the proper control environment
6. Diversity of the firm's operations—products, manufacturing processes
7. High turnover of personnel, especially management personnel
8. Rapid and continual changes in products or services
9. Reporting by operating personnel to nonfinancial managers and a feeling that there is no need to comply with control policies and procedures

10. Resistance by highly technical or creative personnel to control issues
11. Limited staff or budget to support proper control systems
12. Foreign operations
13. Governmental regulations
14. Certain management compensation schemes, based on reported financial results, which create an incentive for biased or incorrect reporting
15. Lack of competence, or a carelessness among record-keeping personnel
16. Large degree of judgment required in accounting records, such as is involved in accounting estimates and in accruals

The auditor can view these characteristics as elements of inherent risk, to the extent that management has not developed a responsive set of control policies and procedures.

Elements of a Sound System of Organizational Controls

The policies and administrative procedures which can make up a sound control system are summarized in the following outline. Exhibit 1 at the end of the chapter presents a more extensive checklist for the review of organizational controls.

1. Policies
   a. Top management commitment to the control system
   b. Establishment of clear areas of responsibility
   c. Company code of ethics
   d. Independence of financial and operating functions
   e. Assurance that financial personnel are knowledgeable of company operations
   f. Maintenance of special oversight for:
      (1) Transactions with related parties
      (2) Management-incentive compensation schemes
   g. Assurance that financial personnel have good, up-to-date accounting backgrounds
   h. Thorough contingency planning and management succession planning
   i. Insurance for facilities; bonding and life insurance for key management personnel
   j. Strong and effective internal audit function
   k. Environment of proper stewardship of the firm's property

2. Procedures
   a. Current job descriptions and organization charts
   b. Work plans, schedules, and manuals
   c. Hiring procedures designed to encourage responsible job performance and to detect the potential for unethical behavior
   d. Continuing education programs for employees
   e. Formal promotion and retention procedures
   f. Reconciliation of articulating records
   g. Centralized accounting systems for payroll and other functions
   h. Measurement systems on all functions
   i. Effective operational and financial audit by the internal audit function
   j. Effective audit committee
   k. Restricted access to vulnerable assets and data

Indicators of a Poor Control Environment

Apart from performing an analysis of the characteristics of the firm and its policies and procedures noted above, the auditor can review the firm's audit history and accounting system for indications of a poor control environment.

Audit History. The results of past audits have a strong impact on the auditor's evaluation of risk. A pattern of audit problems would be associated with greater risk. The problems might be difficulty in dealing with management in obtaining necessary records or in resolving questions about required adjustments to the accounts. If management has been informed of control weaknesses in prior audits and has not responded, one could question its commitment to the control system.

Weakness in the Accounting System. Poor performance of the accounting system can also show lack of commitment to an effective control system. This could be indicated by:

1. Unusually frequent cutoff and accrual errors
2. Lateness or incompleteness of regularly required accounting reports
3. Significant differences between physical inventory and accounting records
4. Inability of accounting personnel to reconcile articulating records or to prepare special analyses (receivables aging, etc.) for the auditor

THE OVERALL EVALUATION OF INHERENT RISK

It is difficult to aggregate all the elements of inherent risk to arrive at an overall evaluation. The four elements we have analyzed are not strictly independent:

1. Operating risk
2. Financial risk
3. Management integrity
4. Organizational control environment

Anything which influences one of the risk elements may thereby also influence one or more of the others. With this in mind, the auditor should consider both the significance of each risk element and the influences between them in making the overall evaluation.

The auditor should not have the view that, since each contributes directly to inherent risk, low risk on one element compensates for high risk on another. On the other hand, the effect on inherent risk is increased substantially when two or more of the elements are rated as high risk. Then the auditor is advised to consider the effect of inherent risk explicitly in audit planning and scope decisions.

FOOTNOTES

[1]Some auditors use the term "general risk" to refer to the three risks collectively.

[2]Others have used the terms "general" or "administrative" to refer to the type of control we call "organizational" control. We use this term to avoid improper interpretation and to emphasize that this control is "organizational" in scope.

[3]SAS 23, paragraph 7(e) states that the auditor must assess the reliability of the industry data used for comparison. "The auditor should consider whether industry information, such as gross margin information, is reasonably available and current and whether data used to compile the information is comparable to the information being evaluated. For example, broad industry information may not be comparable to that of an entity that produces and sells specialized products." The lack of comparability may be a very general problem since research has shown that the financial ratios of firms differ more within broad industry categories than industry average ratios differ among industries (see Trapnell, 1977). Also, the ratios will not be comparable to industry data if the ratios are computed differently among firms within an industry. The lack of uniformity in this context is shown by Charles H. Gibson (1982). Finally, there is the uncertainty concerning how aggregate industry figures are obtained. Are unusual observations ("outliers") deleted or transformed, and so on?

[4]The proper use of ratio analysis is covered in more depth in textbooks on financial

statement analysis. One of the better books of this type is Leopold A. Bernstein, *Financial Statement Analysis* (1978).

[5]Altman and McGough (1974) performed an experiment wherein the results show that the Altman model significantly outperforms unaided auditors in predicting bankruptcy.

[6]Lev and Sunder (1979) present a more thorough discussion of the methodological issues in the use of financial ratios.

[7]Mautz et al. (1980) report survey findings of management's views on the design of effective organizational controls.

[8]See Mautz et al. (1980, p. 44).

REFERENCES

Abdel-Khalik, A. Rashad, and Kamal M. El-Sheshai: "Information Choice and Utilization in an Experiment on Default Prediction," *Journal of Accounting Research,* Autumn 1980, pp. 325–342.

Albrecht, W. Steve, Marshall B. Romney, David J. Cherrington, I. Reed Payne, and Allan J. Roe: *How to Detect and Prevent Business Fraud,* Prentice-Hall, Englewood Cliffs, N.J., 1982.

Altman, Edward: "Financial Ratios, Discriminant Analysis, and the Prediction of Corporate Bankruptcy," *Journal of Finance,* September 1968, pp. 589–609.

———: "Predicting Railroad Bankruptcies in America," *Bell Journal of Economics and Management Science,* Spring 1973, pp. 184–211.

——— and T. McGough: "Evaluation of a Company as a Going Concern," *Journal of Accounting,* December 1974, pp. 50–57.

Backer, Morton, and Martin L. Gosman: *Financial Reporting and Business Liquidity,* National Association of Accountants, 1978.

Beaver, W. H.: "Financial Ratios as Predictors of Failure," *Journal of Accounting Research Supplemental,* 1966, pp. 71–110.

Bernstein, Leopold A.: *Financial Statement Analysis,* rev. ed., Irwin, Homewood, Ill., 1978.

Elliott, Robert K., and John J. Willingham: *Management Fraud: Detection and Deterrence,* Petrocelli, New York, 1980.

Gibson, Charles H.: "How Industry Perceives Financial Ratios," *Management Accounting,* April 1982, pp. 13–19.

Horrigan, James O.: "The Determination of Long-Term Credit Standing with Financial Ratios," *Empirical Research in Accounting: Selected Studies, Journal of Accounting Research,* 1966, pp. 44–62.

Kennedy, Henry A.: "A Behavioral Study of the Usefulness of Four Financial Ratios," *Journal of Accounting Research,* Spring 1975, pp. 97–116.

Largay, James A., III, and Clyde P. Stickney: "Cash Flows, Ratio Analysis and the W. T. Grant Company Bankruptcy," *Financial Analysts Journal,* July–August 1980, pp. 51–54.

Lev, Baruch, and Shyam Sunder: "Methodological Issues in the Use of Financial Ratios," *Journal of Accounting and Economics,* 1979, pp. 189–210.

Mautz, R. K., W. G. Kell, M. W. Maher, A. G. Merten, R. R. Reilly, D. G. Siverance, and B. J. White: *Internal Control in U.S. Corporations: The State of the Art,* Financial Executives Research Foundation, 1980.

Pinches, George E., and Kent A. Mingo: "A Multivariate Analysis of Industrial Bond Ratings," *Journal of Finance,* March 1973, pp. 1–18.

Pogue, Thomas F., and Robert M. Soldofsky: "What's in a Bond Rating," *Journal of Financial and Quantitative Analysis,* June 1969, pp. 201–228.

Ratio Analysis for Small Business, 4th ed., U.S. Small Business Administration Management Series, no. 20, 1977.

Trapnell, Jerry Eugene: "An Empirical Study of the Descriptive Nature of Financial Ratios Relative to Industry Operating Characteristics," unpublished Ph.D. dissertation, University of Georgia, Athens, 1977.

West, Richard R.: "An Alternative Approach to Predicting Corporate Bond Ratings," *Journal of Accounting Research,* Spring 1970, pp. 118–125.

EXHIBIT 1

Checklist for Review of Organizational Controls

A. Personnel policies and relationships
   1. Attitude and involvement of top management
   2. Hiring and promotion of qualified personnel with integrity and high personal ethical standards
   3. Formal training program for financial and accounting personnel
   4. Separation of duties (e.g., between initiation and approval of transactions)
   5. Close, frequent contact with all financial personnel through conferences and personal visits
   6. Good control climate starting at the top

7. Promotion of people to financial management from the internal auditing department

8. Strong dotted-line relationship from CFO of profit centers to corporate CFO

9. Placement of corporate-trained financial people into profit centers

10. Confidentiality of divisional controller's communication to corporate controller

11. Good corporate attitude relating to priorities of soundness, integrity, and proper business ethics in all activities

12. For accountants, an independent role related to controls which transcends responsibility to immediate supervisor

13. One section (or person) controlling or reconciling the activities of another section (or person) within the accounting area

14. No career auditors in corporate internal audit function

15. Training and development programs for all levels of financial and operating management

16. Key senior management with day-to-day operational responsibilities

17. Direct reporting to the corporate office by all division controllers

18. Training for plant controllers and their staffs

B. Special departments, committees, and organizations

1. Systems and methods department

2. Claims adjusters

3. Short and damage freight clerks

4. Separate review committee for special situations

5. Governmental agencies—Defense Contract Audit Agency (DCAA), Air Force (Contractor Management Evaluation Program), SEC, EPA, DOE, NRC

6. Specialized committee system to review, monitor, and control various functions and activities

7. Committee that monitors compliance with internal control procedures and reports periodically to senior management and the audit committee

8. Insurance policy owners examining committee

9. Ethics committee of board of directors

C. Formal systems and procedures

1. Corporate data processing software developed at parent company and processed by a separate subsidiary

2. Standard cost systems with variance analysis

3. Formal systems of delegating the authority to commit funds

4. Computer cost system

5. Expense budgets

    6. Purchasing controls

    7. Physical controls

    8. Order entry system (provides a control over finished goods inventory and entire production and distribution system)

    9. Control of vendor file

  10. Capital budgeting system

  11. Safety and compliance features

  12. Personnel system (controls on hiring and rates of pay)

  13. Detailed financial plan

  14. Central book account for disbursements originating at offices throughout the United States

  15. Strategic and operating management planning and control techniques

  16. Plant physical security

  17. Strategic, intermediate, and 1-year planning activities

D. Instructions, guides, and manuals

    1. Policy statement on internal accounting control

    2. Internal accounting control manual

    3. Statement of levels of authority to approve types of transactions

    4. Operating guidelines for controllers

    5. Financial systems and procedures manual

    6. Personal actions manual

    7. General or corporate policy manual

    8. Accounting manual

    9. System and procedure documentation

  10. Uniform accountancy manual

  11. Corporate finance manual

  12. Supervisory manual

  13. Corporate guidelines for identification of, disposition of, and accounting for obsolete inventory

  14. Corporate policy related to the opening and closing of bank accounts, and the approval and control of checks

  15. Corporate policy relative to the review and approval of contracts

E. Formal and informal practices bearing on internal control

    1. Close examination of personnel reports

    2. Close examination of budget variances

    3. Close examination of travel and entertainment costs

    4. Management involvement in installation, development, maintenance, and use of computer equipment and software

    5. Daily inventory of raw material and finished products

    6. Quality assurance program in controller's department

    7. Two signatures on purchase orders

    8. Blind count of merchandise received

9. Dollar limits on cash purchases by stores
10. Corporate controller approval of bad debt write-off by division
11. Recording of out-of-pattern inventory differences and expense accounts of officers and key employees
12. Subjection of operating unit controllers to salary administration by the corporate controller
13. Detailed budgets
14. Observation of internal control of subsidiaries by service people from corporate office
15. Review of results of all internal and external audits by and with subsidiary presidents
16. Joint custody over negotiable securities
17. Presentation of defalcation reports to audit committee
18. Task force teams for special control problems
19. Extensive comparisons with other companies in same business of the same size
20. Management committees
21. Minutes of meetings
22. Audits by outside contractors
23. Close coordination between external and internal auditors
24. Uniform chart of accounts
25. Audits by manufacturer and financial institutions
26. Active audit committee (10 meetings a year)
27. Involvement of EDP auditors with financial and manufacturing system design

F. Regular reviews and representations
1. Corporate controller's review of operating companies' balance sheets
2. Internal control questionnaire
3. Questionable payments review
4. Representation letters from operating management and controllers
5. Circularization of findings of internal and external auditors
6. Annual certification of adequacy of internal control system
7. Monthly corporate review of divisional operations
8. Irregular check of all payroll authorizations
9. Examination of certain employees' and all officers' income tax returns
10. Monthly management checklist signed by division general managers and controllers
11. Annual formal report of audit committee (quality, hours, achievements, etc.)
12. Certification concerning misuse of corporate bonds

13. Annual self-audit by each unit manager
14. Certification concerning conflict of interest
15. Quarterly audits by the external auditor
16. Weekly meetings of top management to discuss changes in financial outlook
17. Quarterly and annual detailed analyses of accounts and significant judgment items
18. Quarterly evaluation of investments
G. Special one-time actions
    1. Three-year program to review, reevaluate, and document internal accounting controls
    2. Analysis and documentation of existing controls
H. Recurring reports
    1. Monthly labor ratio reports by operating unit
    2. Operating cost reports
    3. Activity reports
    4. Weekly profit and loss statements
    5. Weekly labor utilization reports
    6. Weekly raw material yield reports
    7. Daily general ledger
    8. Internal accounting newsletter
I. Financial policies
    1. Specific levels of approval for capital expenditures
    2. Bonding of all employees and agents
    3. Manual signature of any two of several designated officers for any check over $10,000

SOURCE: Adapted from Mautz et al. (1980, pp. 32–38).

chapter
three

Trend
Analysis

"I hold that man is in the right who is most closely in league with the future."

Letters of Henrik Ibsen

Trend analysis is the most commonly used of all analytical review procedures. It is the analysis of the changes in a given account balance, item, or element over the past accounting periods, usually annual periods. In some instances the analysis is a simple comparison of the prior year's balance to the current balance. Or, it may involve a more complex analysis of the 12 to 36 or more monthly figures preceding the current balance. The latter approach usually involves statistical time-series methods of analysis.

Our objective in this chapter is to deal principally with those types of analyses which can be done with pencil and paper and require a dozen or fewer time-series observations. The more complex statistical methods are identified and explained, and a thorough development of the technical aspects of these methods is presented, in Appendix 4.

The most common form of trend analysis is the comparison of current and prior years, based either on the annual figures alone or on a pairwise comparison of the monthly figures in each year. Since this technique is so well known, we will not explain and illustrate it. Rather, the objective of this chapter is to describe a variety of different forms of trend analysis, some of which the auditor may find provide a new and useful approach in certain audit situations. Also, we are concerned about the relative effectiveness of the different types of trend analysis and the potential for judgment errors that might be associated with them. In essence, the objectives of the chapter are threefold.

1.   The first objective is to describe a wide variety of trend analysis procedures, all of which are easy to understand and simple to apply. The auditor's choice of a procedure will depend on the nature and quality of the data available.

2.   The second objective is to provide guidance for the auditor in choosing a cutoff point for determining when the current amount is, or is not, out of line with the past trend. The cutoff can be expressed either as a percentage of the current amount or as a given dollar amount. The choice of a cutoff is based in part upon materiality considerations and upon guidelines of authoritative bodies, such as the AICPA and SEC.

3.   The third objective is to present information from prior research findings about the auditor's tendency to make certain judgment mistakes when using trend analysis. These mistakes often come about because of a lack of understanding of the nature of the actual relationship over time between various financial statement accounts. Also, research has shown that the decision maker's use of time-series data is subject to certain consistent and well-known biases. An awareness of these mistakes and biases can help the auditor to use trend analysis most effectively.

ELEMENTS OF EFFECTIVE USE OF TREND ANALYSIS

Apart from the choice of trend analysis techniques, which we analyze in the following section, the auditor must apply a proper understanding of each of the four elements of effective trend analysis:

Use a Causal Approach

In trend analysis, the auditor uses either a *causal* or a *diagnostic* approach. The causal approach is one wherein the auditor answers the question "What should the amount be this year?" That is, the auditor gives a prediction explicitly, basing it upon the trend of the data. In contrast, using the diagnostic approach the auditor simply compares the current amount with the past trend to determine if it appears to be out of line; no explicit prediction is involved. This is called the "diagnostic" approach because it can be compared to a physician's looking for a symptom of disease; if there is no symptom, then the physician concludes there is no disease. Unfortunately, in accounting and auditing matters, items which may appear OK (i.e., show no symptoms) can be significantly misstated. Thus, a causal approach is recommended. The auditor develops an understanding of what "causes" the trend of the account analyzed, uses this to make a prediction of the amount, and then compares predicted with reported amounts. Only in this way can the auditor detect a potential problem in an account for which there is little or no change from the prior period, but where there should have been a significant change because of changes in the related causal factors.

For example, consider the following hypothetical case. A supplies inventory balance had changed little from the prior year, yet significant quantity increases for these items had occurred. Upon investigation, the auditor discovered that the inventory clerk had failed to include the contents of a new stockroom in the year-end inventory count, thereby significantly understating the supplies inventory and overstating supplies expense. The causal approach probably would have detected the problem, by taking the inventory expansion explicitly into account. The diagnostic approach probably would have missed the problem because of the lack of a "symptom."

Because it requires more effort, the causal approach is more costly, so the auditor considers the cost-benefit of the two approaches, as well as the audit risk and materiality involved, when choosing an audit approach.

Evaluate Prediction Error

The potential for prediction error is implicit in the diagnostic approach but explicit in the causal approach. Trend analysis is fundamentally a process of prediction and judgment, so that the evaluation of prediction error is an important part of the process. As for any financial forecast, the auditor evaluates the potential for error in trend analysis by considering the quality of the process by which the prediction is made:

1.   To what extent is an in-depth knowledge of the operating environment of the auditee incorporated in the prediction process? How well does the auditor understand the auditee's business and its operations?
2.   How predictable are the operating characteristics of the auditee? The accounts for a mature company in a stable industry are the most easily understood and predicted, while in contrast the growing company in an unstable industry represents an inherently less predictable situation.
3.   Certain trend analysis techniques are more accurate than others because they use more data or more precise statistical procedures.

Our approach for the evaluation of prediction error is presented later in this chapter. As noted above, certain trend analysis techniques offer greater accuracy than others. This in turn allows the auditor greater reliance on the technique and thereby a potentially greater reduction in the extent of other planned substantive texts.

Evaluate Reliability of Data

Because it directly affects the accuracy of the trend analysis, the reliability of the data employed is an important audit concern. Nonfinancial data present a particular problem in this regard since the auditor does not ordinarily evaluate the auditee's controls for the reliability of these types of data. Also, the auditor may use external sources of data for industry or general economic variables. While some of these sources are known to be reliable—such as Standard and Poor's, Dun and Bradstreet, Moody's, Robert Morris Associates, and others—there is little known about the reliability of the many other sources which the auditor may require in any given audit situation. For example, data on local economic activity may be especially relevant for a trend analysis, yet very little may be known about the reliability of the sources for such data (various chambers of commerce, etc). The auditor considers the effect of the untested reliability of these sources on the trend analysis—it enhances the potential for prediction error.

Provide Proper Follow-Up

The final element of an effective trend analysis is the proper follow-up in those cases in which the analysis indicates further investigation is warranted. The follow-up is subject to the same criteria for audit evidence as for any other audit procedure. That is, the follow-up must produce evidence that is relevant and persuasive. The common approach of inquiry of management to explain significant fluctuations is appropriate, but the auditor should consider whether certain of management's assertions should be independently verified.

TECHNIQUES FOR TREND ANALYSIS

The techniques for trend analysis can be conveniently categorized as either single- or multiple-variable models.[1] The single-variable model is one such that the predicted amount is based only upon the prior time-series data for that account. The prediction of sales revenue from the prior 36 months' sales figures is an example. In contrast, the multiple-variable model, while providing a prediction for a single variable, will use time-series data for two or more variables in the prediction process. A common representation of the multiple-variable model is the time-series regression model, where the dependent variable is the predicted amount and the independent variable or variables are the one or more predictors for which time-series data are available. Both models are commonly applied in trend analysis for analytical review.

The distinction between these two classes of techniques is important, because the nature of the techniques differs substantially. Thus, the following discussion presents them separately. Greater attention is given to the single-variable model because it is more easily done by the unaided auditor; multiple-variable models often require the use of a computer.

Single-Variable Techniques

In describing the techniques for single variables we proceed from the simplest to the most complex. The more complex the technique is, the more accurate are its predictions generally. However, more complex techniques will also require a greater commitment of audit resources—auditor expertise and time, data gathering, and so on. Thus, our approach presents a menu of available techniques from which the auditor can choose, according to the needs of each audit situation. There are five types of single-variable techniques:

1. Graphical method
2. Period-to-period change method
3. Weighted average method
4. Moving average method
5. Statistical time-series analysis

Throughout the following discussion we will refer to the account, item, or element that the auditor is predicting as the "predicted variable" or "dependent variable."

The Graphical Method. The first technique attempts to gain insight into the trend of the predicted variable by visual inspection of graphic data. This is done in one of three ways. The simplest of the three is to construct what is called a "scatter diagram" by plotting the data over time. To illustrate, the time-series sales data in column 2 of Table 3-1 is plotted in a scatter diagram in Figure 3-1. Using the scatter diagram, the auditor is able to determine the sales pattern visually and thereby project sales for the coming year. For this illustration, if the auditor feels the overall upward trend in sales will continue, then a prediction for 1984 should lie somewhere between $700,000 and $825,000. The upper and lower dashed lines are used to help predict by showing visually the boundaries within which recent years' sales amounts have fallen. The auditor would then use his or her knowledge of the economic prospects of the firm to come up with a single-value prediction. Using a "freehanded" prediction line as shown, we find that a reasonable prediction for 1984 sales would be $750,000. The $700,000 to $825,000 range can be interpreted as a "confidence interval" for the prediction, to reflect its degree of precision.

This visual-fit approach has three limitations. One is the limited precision of the estimate; unless the pattern of the data is very regular, the auditor's confidence interval is likely to be large, as in the above illustration. Another limitation is the influence on the prediction of one or more very unusual data observations. These could bias the prediction significantly, so the auditor must consider whether these observations are a valid part of the overall pattern of the data. If not, they should be omitted from the scatter diagram.

The final limitation we will discuss is the potential bias due to the auditor's choice of scale for the scatter diagram. For example, Figure 3-2 reproduces the data in Figure 3-1 using a more compressed scale for the sales axis. The visual effect of the two figures is quite different: Figure 3-1 enhances the trend to the data and Figure 3-2 dampens it. The auditor then must consider this "scale effect" in determining the prediction and confidence interval.

One approach to avoiding the scale effect would be for the auditor to use the same type of graph paper on all engagements, and to scale every graph for an engagement in units of the materiality figure used for that engagement.

To add precision to the graphical approach, the auditor can use a simple algebraic calculation to determine the equation for a straight line

Table 3-1 DBB Company Sales

Year (1)	Sales, $ (2)	Change in Sales (3)	% Change in Sales (4)	Rank (5)	Weighted % Change* (6)	Weighted Absolute† Change (7)	Exponential Smoothed Sales, $‡ (8)	Exponential Smoothed % Change‡ (9)	Exponential Smoothed Sales, $§ (10)	Exponential Smoothed % Change§ (11)
1977	361,936									
1978	400,776	$ 38,840	1.107	1	1.107	$ 38,840	381,356	—	393,008	
1979	518,609	117,833	1.294	2	2.588	235,666	449,983	1.201	493,489	1.257
1980	592,314	73,705	1.142	3	3.426	221,115	521,149	1.171	572,549	1.165
1981	553,047	−39,267	0.934	4	3.736	−157,608	536,809	1.053	556,947	0.980
1982	668,636	115,589	1.209	5	6.045	577,945	602,722	1.131	646,298	1.163
1983	645,901	−22,735	.966	6	5.796	−136,410	624,312	1.048	645,980	1.005
		$283,965	6.652	21	22.698	$779,548				
		÷ 6	÷ 6		÷ 21	÷ 21				
		$ 47,328	1.109		1.081	$ 37,121				

*(6) = (4) × (5).
†(7) = (3) × (5).
‡α = 0.5.
§α = 0.8.

53

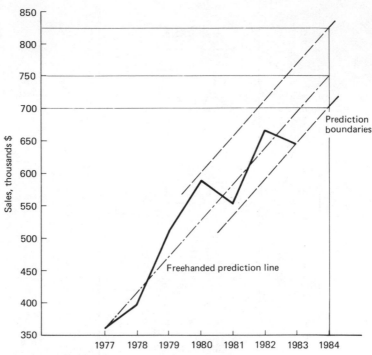

Figure 3-1   DBB Company sales—scatter diagram.

which fits the data points. This quick calculation frees the auditor from the scale effect and helps to reduce the problem associated with very unusual data observations. The algebraic method also provides a prediction equation which contributes mathematical precision to the prediction. The equation is

$$X = a + bT$$

where X = value of the predicted amount—in this case, sales (vertical axis)

   T = variable representing the time dimension (horizontal axis)

   a = fixed quantity which represents the value of X when $T = 0$ (the intersection of the vertical axis and the straight line)

   b = slope of the line, that is, the change in sales per unit change in time

   To obtain the equation, the auditor first draws through the data points a freehand line which best fits the overall pattern of the data. An example of this is shown in Figure 3-1. The auditor then chooses two

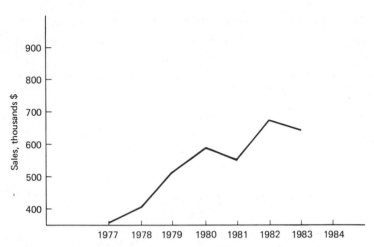

Figure 3-2   DBB Company sales—compressed scatter diagram.

points which are both close to the freehand line and a year or two apart—in this case, the sales amounts for 1978 and 1981 would be a good choice. Then

$$b = \frac{\$553,047 - \$400,776}{5 - 2} = \$50,757$$

(Assume 1981 = year 5 and 1978 = year 2.)

$$a = X - bT = \$553,047 - \$50,757 \times 5 = \$299,262$$

and then $X = \$299,262 + \$50,757T$

Using this equation, the predicted sales for 1984 (year 8) is

Sales (1984) = \$299,262 + \$50,757 \times 8 = \$705,318

Upon inspection, it is clear that this algebraic model, since it is linear, states that the best prediction for sales is a $50,757 increase over the prior year, for any year.

The Period-to-Period Change Method.   This method is one of the most commonly used in current audit practice. When properly applied, it can provide very good predictions. It involves an algebraic calculation of the trend in a data series, based on changes between one or more prior periods of data.

It is convenient for us at this point to introduce some mathematical notation to help describe this method:

X_T = *actual* value of the balance, item, or element in period T

X_{T-1} = *actual* value of the balance, item, or element in the period prior to period T

$\hat{X}_{T+1}$ = *predicted* value of the balance, item, or element in the period following period T

$\hat{X}_{T-2}$, $\hat{X}_{T-3}$, . . . are defined in a similar fashion.

Now, the auditor can use either the *absolute amount* of change from prior to current period, or the *rate* of change from prior to current period, to predict the next period, as follows:

$$\hat{X}_{T+1} = X_T + (X_T - X_{T-1}) \qquad \text{(absolute change method)}$$

$$\hat{X}_{T+1} = X_T \left(\frac{X_T}{X_{T-1}}\right) \qquad \text{(rate of change method)}$$

To illustrate, with the data in Table 3-1

Predicted sales (1984) = sales (1983) + [sales (1983) − sales (1982)]

= \$645,901 + (\$645,901 − \$668,636)

= \$623,166   (absolute change method)

or

Predicted sales (1984) = sales (1983) × $\dfrac{\text{sales (1983)}}{\text{sales (1982)}}$

= \$645,901 × $\dfrac{\$645,901}{668,636}$

= \$623,939   (rate of change method)

Two aspects of these prediction methods are readily apparent. First, they produce comparable predictions, which is generally the case for these methods. Both models predict well when the underlying time series is approximately linear, though the absolute change model will generally outperform the other. However, when the underlying time series has a trend that is somewhat faster (or slower) than linear, then the absolute change model will underestimate (or overestimate) the correct amount and the degree of error is directly proportional to the extent that the trend departs from the linear in either direction. On the other hand, the rate of change method always overestimates, regardless of trend, and the degree of error is always higher than for the absolute change method. Thus, the auditor will be better served in most cases by the absolute change model; the rate of change method is used only when the auditor's knowledge of the data indicates it is the superior method.

A second observation about the above illustration is that both methods, by construction, cannot "see" the direction of the trend beyond that given by the two most recent data points. Thus, since the two most recent data points in Table 3-1 indicate a downward trend, the predictions for both period-to-period change methods are quite low relative to the predictions of either the visual-fit method or the equation method shown earlier. The auditor can adapt the period-to-period change method to a larger number of data points by averaging the changes over the last few periods, say, n periods in general. Then, the predicted amounts are as follows:

$$\hat{X}_{T+1} = X_T + \frac{\sum_{i=0}^{n} [X_{T-i} - X_{T-(i+1)}]}{n+1} \qquad \text{(absolute change method)}$$

$$\hat{X}_{T+1} = X_T \left[\sum_{i=0}^{n} \frac{X_{T-i}}{X_{T-(i+1)}} \right] \frac{1}{n+1} \qquad \text{(rate of change method)}$$

For the data in Table 3-1 (refer to columns 3 and 4)

Predicted sales (1984) = \$645,901 + \$47,328

= \$693,229 (absolute change method)

or

Predicted sales (1984) = \$645,901 × 1.109

= \$716,304 (rate of change method)

Finally, the period-to-period change method can also be adapted to account for seasonal fluctuations in the data, should the auditor want a prediction for a month or a quarter. For example, if there is a stable seasonal pattern from year to year, then where the period T is a month

$$\hat{X}_{T+1} = X_{T-11} + (X_{T-11} - X_{T-23}) \qquad \text{(absolute change method)}$$

$$\hat{X}_{T+1} = X_{T-11} \left(\frac{X_{T-11}}{X_{T-23}} \right) \qquad \text{(rate of change method)}$$

These formulas would incorporate both a seasonal effect and an annual trend for a month-by-month prediction.

The Weighted Average Method. The auditor may consider the above approach deficient in some cases because it weights each period's data equally. The auditor may in these cases wish to have the more recent observations weighted more heavily in the prediction, since the more recent data are more relevant. This is easily done once the weights are assigned. Of course, choosing how to assign the weights to the periods is a matter for experienced judgment; there is no single acceptable way to do it. One common approach is simply to rank the periods 1, 2, . . . and so on from least to most recent. To illustrate, consider again the data in Table 3-1. Columns 5, 6, and 7 illustrate the weighted average method using the simple ranking of years. The predictions are as follows:

Predicted sales (1984) = $645,901 + $37,121 (absolute change method)
= $683,022

Predicted sales (1984) = $645,901 × 1.081   (rate of change method)
= $698,219

Note that the predicted sales figures for the weighted average approach are slightly lower than those of the unweighted averaging method shown earlier. The reason for this is that the weighted average methods emphasize the most recent years, and the data in column 2 of Table 3-1 have relatively lower average increases in the most recent years.

The Moving Average Method.   Another method for giving greater weight to more recent observations is the moving average method. This method is especially useful when monthly or quarterly predictions are required because it is able to handle seasonal fluctuations conveniently and is easily updated for new data. We consider two ways the auditor can apply a moving average approach:

1.   Unweighted moving average
2.   Exponential smoothing (weighted moving average)

We illustrate first the unweighted moving average method, again by reference to the data in Table 3-1. A distinguishing characteristic of this method is that it requires the auditor to evaluate the length of any cyclical pattern of the data. For example, by inspecting Table 3-1 or Figure 3-1 the auditor might conclude that, in recent years, there has been approximately a 2-year cycle to the data. That is, there is an up-and-down cycle for the period 1982–1983. The 2-year cycle is then the base for the computation of the unweighted moving average used in the forecast

$$\text{Predicted sales (1984)} = \$645,901 + \frac{\$115,589 - 22,735}{2} \quad \text{(absolute}$$
$$= \$692,328 \qquad \text{change method)}$$

$$\text{or} \quad \text{Predicted sales (1984)} = \$645,901 \times \frac{1.209 + .966}{2} \quad \text{(rate of}$$
$$= \$702,417 \qquad \text{change method)}$$

This approach is called the moving average method because the average for each cycle length includes the most recent data; that is, the average "moves" forward and is updated as new data are added. In effect, this method provides a smoothed prediction by averaging over seasonal and cyclical fluctuations. Again, the averaging period is chosen so as to match the length of fluctuations in the data. If the data are stable with small fluctuations, then the averging period can be large. In this case we have something that resembles the period-to-period method described earlier. But, if significant fluctuations are present, the averaging period should be short and match the period of fluctuations.[2]

The second type of moving average includes a weighting of past data and is called "exponential smoothing." As we shall see, it also offers certain computational efficiencies over the unweighted approach. A key characteristic of the exponential smoothing method is that a smoothed value must be obtained for both the data series itself and the trend for the data series; that is, this method separates the two aspects of the data—the trend and the fluctuations about the trend. To continue with the sample data in Table 3-1, the exponential smoothing method forecasts in the following way:[3]

$$\text{Predicted sales (1984)} = \text{smoothed sales (1983)}$$
$$\times \text{smoothed trend (1983)}$$

Our meaning for "trend" is simply the percentage change from year to year, as given in column 4 of Table 3-1. We consider now how the smoothing is done.

The term "smoothing" is used to reflect that this method averages over the fluctuations in the data in such a way that more recent periods are weighted more heavily than later periods. The weighting is done by a geometric series of the following form, where α is the weighting constant:

$$1, (1-\alpha), (1-\alpha)^2, \ldots$$

The constant α is a number between 0 and 1, so that weights in the sequence of terms above become progressively smaller. Suppose $\alpha = 0.5$; then the smoothed value of a time series at time T is given by the following, where $S(X_T)$ represents the smoothed value of the series X at time T.

$$S(X_T) = \frac{X_T + \frac{1}{2}X_{T-1} + \frac{1}{4}X_{T-2}}{1 + \frac{1}{2} + \frac{1}{4}}$$

The smoothing goes back as many periods as good data are available, each period being weighted less than the one before. Using algebra, we are able to simplify the above equation, to give the following, which is called the smoothing function

$$S(X_T) = \alpha X_T + (1 - \alpha)[S(X_{T-1})]$$

That is, the smoothed value at time T is a linear combination of the actual value at time T and the smoothed value of the prior period. Look again at Table 3-1 for an illustration of the smoothing function. Column 8 shows the smoothed figures for sales using a weighting of $\alpha = 0.5$. For example, the smoothed sales for 1978 and 1979 are computed as follows:

Smoothed sales (1979)
$$= \tfrac{1}{2} \text{ actual sales (1979)} + \tfrac{1}{2} \text{ smoothed sales (1978)}$$
$$= \tfrac{1}{2} \times \$518,609 + \tfrac{1}{2} \times \$381,356$$
$$= \$449,983$$

and

Smoothed sales (1978) $= \tfrac{1}{2} \times \$400,776 + \tfrac{1}{2} \times \$361,936$
$$= \$381,356$$

The actual sales for 1977 were used in this latter computation since 1977 is the first data period, and thus smoothed sales for 1977 cannot be computed. The smoothing function is applied in a similar manner for all periods, and for the percentage change figures in column 4 as well as for sales. The result is the smoothed figures in columns 8 and 9, which are used to predict sales for 1984.

Predicted sales (1984)
$$= \text{smoothed sales (1983)} \times \text{smoothed trend (1983)}$$
$$= \$624,312 \times 1.048$$
$$= \$654,278$$

The above prediction has used a weighting constant value of $\alpha = 0.5$, which is the midpoint of all possible values, α being between 0 and 1. The choice of this value is part of the prediction process, and it will affect the resulting prediction. The value of α can be compared to the cycle length used in the moving average method. That is, the smaller α is, the greater the impact of distant periods' data on the smoothed prediction. Conversely, the larger α is, the greater the relative impact of more recent observations. Thus, a small α is generally more appropriate for a stable time series, while a large α is more suitable for a time series with significant fluctuations. When α is large, the smoothed prediction responds rapidly to changes in trend.

The auditor may choose to compute the smoothed prediction with two or three different values for α and evaluate the results.[4] If significantly different predictions are obtained, the auditor may choose to study the time series further to obtain a better understanding of the factors influencing the fluctuations, and then choose the best prediction. To illustrate, if the data in Table 3-1 are smoothed using α = 0.8, the resulting prediction, using columns 10 and 11, would be:

Predicted sales (1984) = $645,980 × 1.005 = $649,210

This prediction differs little from that of the α = 0.5 model, so that a small range around $650,000 appears to provide a reasonably precise prediction using the exponential smoothing method.

Statistical Time-Series Analysis. A complete discussion of the available statistical techniques for trend analysis is beyond the scope of the book. Such a discussion would necessarily be quite technical in nature and would presume a high level of understanding of statistical terms, concepts, and techniques. Thus, our approach is to describe these techniques in a general way at this point and to present in Appendix 4 a more in-depth discussion of one of the techniques, regression analysis. The two statistical techniques available for trend analysis are regression analysis and Box-Jenkins (B-J) time-series analysis.

Regression analysis is a statistical technique for finding a best-fit trend line for a series of observations. It can be compared to the algebra-equation technique illustrated earlier in connection with the graphical method. This technique uses the equation $X = a + bT$, where X is the predicted amount, T is a variable representing time, and the constants a and b are as defined earlier. The algebra-equation technique provides good estimates of a and b, using only two data points. In contrast, the regression method would use all seven data points in the example cited earlier, and thus finds that unique set of constants (a and b) which minimizes prediction error. Therefore, the regression line generally provides a better fit than does the algebra-equation technique.[5] Consult Appendix 4 for the development of how this is done mathematically.

When regression analysis is applied to the data in Table 3-1, the following equation results, where $T = 7$ means 1983, and so on:

Sales = $331,312 + 50,787$T$

Thus   Predicted sales (1984) = $331,312 + $50,787 × 8

= $737,608

The benefits of the regression approach are the mathematical precision of the prediction, since it provides the best-fit prediction line, and the fact that it uses all available data. However, it does not pick up fluctuating patterns and changes in trend as do the period-to-period change and moving average methods. The auditor uses an understanding of the past behavior of the time series to help choose which prediction method to use.

Another statistical approach, which is a good deal more complex than regression analysis but which will pick up fluctuating patterns to the data, is the B-J method. This is a statistical technique which develops very good predictions by extracting the statistical properties of the time-series data over many observations. The B-J method actually consists of many different prediction techniques—simple trend models, smoothing models, and so on. The B-J prediction is based on the best-fitting of all these models.

Multiple-Variable Techniques

The multiple-variable model is most easily described by reference to our prediction equation, as defined for regression, $X = a + bT$. If we replace T with a series of data for a new variable (Z) which is related in some way to the predicted variable (X), then we have a multiple-variable model. The variable Z is called the "independent" (predictor) variable, while X is called the "dependent" (predicted) variable. We then must have data for each variable $(X$ and $Z)$ for each of the T time periods. The two types of models are contrasted in Figure 3-3.

For example, suppose the sales data in Table 3-1, column 2, represent investment income (X) rather than sales for our audit client. And, we know that the value of investments (Z) is a good predictor of investment income. The data for this new variable are given in the accompanying table. Now, we can obtain our prediction for X by developing the prediction equation

$$X_T = a + bZ_T$$

We can find the values for the constants a and b in the same manner as

	Independent Variable (z): Value of Investment, thousands $
1977	6,325
1978	7,001
1979	7,360
1980	7,636
1981	7,215
1982	7,789
1983	8,014

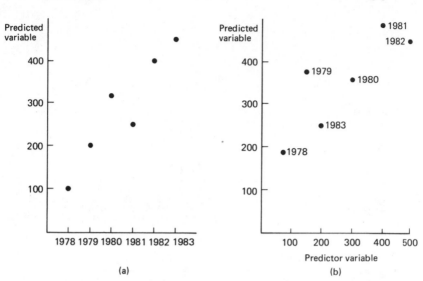

Figure 3-3 Illustrations of (*a*) single- and (*b*) multiple-variable analysis.

we have for the single-variable cases presented earlier—by the algebra-equation method or through regression analysis. The period-to-period change and moving average methods no longer apply.

Algebra-Equation Method.   The values for the constants a and b are computed as follows (the data for the years 1977 and 1980 are selected on the basis of an examination of a scatter diagram, Figure 3-4):

$$b = \frac{592.314 - 361.936}{7636 - 6325} = 0.176$$

$$a = X - bZ = \$592,314 - 0.176 \times \$7,636,000 = -\$751,622$$

and

$$X = -\$751,622 + 0.176 \times Z$$

Thus, if 1984 investments were \$8,260,000 we would predict investment income as

Predicted income (1984) = −\$751,622 + 0.176 × \$8,260,000
                                    = \$702,138

This figure can be compared with the reported income figure for reasonableness.

Linear Regression Method.   Applying a linear regression ap-

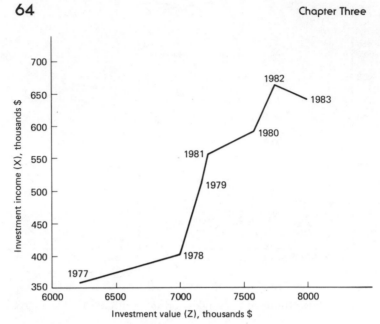

Figure 3-4   Investment income versus investment value.

proach to these data gives similar results. The regression equation computed by the methods described in Appendix 4 is as follows:

$$X = -\$872,955 + 0.192 \times Z$$

and   Predicted income (1984) $= -\$872,955 + 0.192 \times \$8,260,000$
$$= \$712,965$$

Again, the benefit associated with the regression approach is the greater accuracy of the prediction which comes from the mathematics involved. Also, it is possible when using regression to employ two or more predictor variables rather than the one predictor used in the above illustration. The use of an additional predictor variable can enhance the accuracy of the prediction. For example, the auditor could use data about interest rates as a second predictor variable in the above illustration. Assuming interest rates are relevant, the resulting prediction should be more accurate when both the investment amount and interest rates are used.

Use Care When Making the Prediction.   When making the prediction by either the equation or the regression method, the auditor should consider three potential causes of inaccurate predictions:

1. *Inaccurate data.*
2. *Unstable pattern to the data.* If the data fluctuate significantly or do not

have a single discernible trend, then neither of these methods will always give good results. In such cases the auditor should avoid placing too much reliance on the prediction.

3. *Improper model.* An improper model is one where the predicted and predictor variables, which are assumed to be related, are in fact not related at all or are only weakly related. The auditor has chosen the wrong predictor variable for the equation or regression. Also, the relationship might be nonlinear, rather than the assumed linear form. The auditor can avoid such errors by developing a good understanding of the variable being predicted. What other financial and operating data time series are strongly related to the one being predicted? And, what is the proper form of the relationship?

Computer Software

An increasing number of auditors have ready access to a computer or computer service, a situation which makes possible the use of planning and forecasting software for trend analysis. Many of these software packages are available on microcomputers, thus enhancing portability and reducing cost. The auditor can use the packages to complete the complex and tedious arithmetic associated with many of the techniques discussed in this chapter. The packages commonly include such features as moving averages, exponential smoothing, seasonal and cyclical adjustment, regression analysis, and in some cases the Box-Jenkins time-series analysis. Among the most well known of these packages are the following (there are many others):

STATPRO	Wadsworth Electronic Publishing Company 20 Park Plaza Boston, MA 02116 (617) 423-0420
MICRO-DSS/Analysis	Addison-Wesley Publishing Company Reading, MA 01867 (617) 944-3700
MICRO-TSP	McGraw-Hill Book Company 1221 Avenue of the Americas New York, NY 10020 (212) 512-6611
FAST	Financial Audit Systems 3801 Wake Forest Rd., Suite 204 Raleigh, NC 27609 (919) 876-5033

STATPAC   Walonick Associates, Inc.
                                 5624 Girard Avenue South
                                 Minneapolis, MN 55419
                                 (512) 866-9022

Of course, the auditor may also engage a specialized consultant to
develop a forecasting package tailored to the auditor's particular needs.

ESTIMATION OF PREDICTION ERROR

A critical aspect of the effective use of trend analysis is the auditor's
explicit consideration of the potential amount of prediction error. That
is, what is the range above and below the predicted amount in which the
auditor is fairly confident the actual value will be? This interval will be
relatively wide in those cases when the auditor is not very confident of
the prediction, and narrower for more confident predictions. The
determination of this prediction interval is most often a subjective
matter. Only the statistical methods, such as regression, produce objective measures of potential prediction error.[6] Thus, the auditor will most
often feel somewhat frustrated trying to estimate the prediction error.

Our approach is to have the auditor express his or her judgment
about the potential error, whether in numerical terms or in qualitative
terms. For example, the auditor might give the upper and lower values
of the interval within which he or she feels the actual value will lie, with
some stated confidence. Alternatively, the auditor might simply say the
potential for prediction error is "high" or "low." The point of this
judgment process is to enhance the auditor's awareness of the importance of incorporating an assessment of potential prediction error in
using a trend analysis. The more precise the judgment can be, the better
the auditor is able to determine how much reliance to place on it.

THE AUDITOR'S DECISION

This section presents some of the available research about auditor
judgment in trend analysis. It should serve as a guide for the individual
auditor in using trend analysis more effectively. The discussion focuses
on what we know about the tendencies, or "biases," which the auditor,
knowingly or not, applies when using trend analysis.

For the purposes of this section, we consider the auditor's decision to be two-phased—(1) whether to investigate any particular account or item (the "attention-directing" function of trend analysis) and (2) how far to push the investigation, once initiated. We do not consider here auditor judgments about reducing tests of details as the result of analytical review procedures.

One important consideration when deciding whether to investigate an account or item is determining the "cutoff" dollar amount or percent difference between predicted and reported amounts beyond which an investigation should be undertaken. This cutoff amount or percent is generally related to materiality for the engagement. Our research on senior-level auditors has shown that a cutoff of 5 percent of net income before tax or 10 percent of net income after tax is a good approximation for the rule most commonly applied by these auditors. However, this is an average figure, and auditors differ somewhat on the cutoff applied. On the other hand, each auditor tends to apply a chosen cutoff consistently when going from one audit situation to another.

Our studies also show that the direction of the difference (predicted minus reported) does not seem to affect the auditor's choice of a cutoff. That is, auditors appear to treat the over- and underprediction cases pretty much in an equivalent manner. Also, the auditors tend to base their investigation decisions on the dollar amount differences rather than the percentage difference itself; that is, the amount of the difference (predicted minus reported amount) is the key element of the investigation decision.

Another study has shown that the auditor's determination of a cutoff may be improperly influenced by the current unaudited amount. When determining a prediction interval wherein the actual value probably lies, the auditors may center the interval on the unaudited amount rather than the predicted amount. This implies indirectly a bias to accept the unaudited amount since it is at the center of the prediction interval. It also suggests that auditors are using the unaudited value in making the prediction for the amount, which again biases the auditor to accept the unaudited amount.

This tendency to focus on the unaudited amount is a judgment bias common to many judgment tasks—in business, medicine, and other areas. It has been called the "confirmation bias," since it reflects the decision maker's tendency *not* to seek out disconfirming evidence; that is, a diagnostic approach is taken rather than a causal approach. Time pressure can increase the tendency to this bias, though the natural skepticism displayed by auditors acts to reduce it. In all, the auditor must be alert to the effects of his or her own tendency to the confirmation bias, because research has shown that it is a common human trait.

Another set of studies we have reviewed seems to show that decision makers and auditors have a tendency to perceive a trend to a series of data when no trend is present. Or, when a trend is present, they will overestimate its strength. This also appears to be a common characteristic of human judgment and perception, and auditors should be alert to the effects of the bias in their own trend analysis judgments.

FOOTNOTES

[1]Useful references for trend analysis techniques are the texts by Gross and Peterson (1976) and Chisholm and Whitaker (1971).

[2]One of the well-known properties of the unweighted moving average method, especially for longer averaging periods, is the tendency to indicate a cyclical pattern to the data where none is present. By a "cycle" we mean a fluctuation which extends over many months, in contrast to a seasonal fluctuation, over a relatively few months. The auditor should keep this in mind when using four or more periods in the moving average.

[3]A more in-depth treatment of the exponential smoothing forecasting technique is available in Chisholm and Whitaker (1971, pp. 22–26).

[4]The single best value for α, that which gives the least prediction error over the past data, can be determined by statistical methods such as regression. The regression method is developed fully in the Appendix 4.

[5]Hogarth and Makridakis (1981) compare the performance of simple and complex prediction models, and report that the simple models perform as well as or better than the complex models more often than most forecasters realize. Also, Makridakis and Winkler (1983) show that prediction accuracy can be improved by averaging the predictions of two or more different methods.

[6]In regression, the measure of the confidence interval for the prediction is called the "standard error of the estimate." The computation and interpretation of the standard error of the estimate are presented in Appendix 4.

REFERENCES

Albrecht, W. S.: "Toward Better and More Efficient Audits," *Journal of Accountancy,* December 1978, pp. 49–50.

_____ and J. C. McKeown: "Toward an Extended Use of Statistical Analytical Reviews in the Audit," *Proceedings of the University of Illinois Audit Symposium,* University of Illinois, 1977.

Chisholm, Roger K., and Gilbert R. Whitaker, Jr.: *Forecasting Methods,* Irwin, Homewood, Ill., 1971.

Geurts, Michael D., and Thomas A. Buchman: "Accounting for 'Shocks' in Forecasts," *Management Accounting,* April 1981, pp. 21–39.

Gross, Charles W., and Robin T. Peterson: *Business Forecasting,* Houghton Mifflin, Boston, 1976.

Hogarth, Robin M., and Spyros Makridakis: "Forecasting and Planning: An Evaluation," *Management Science,* February 1981, pp. 115–138.

Kaplan, Robert S.: "Developing a Financial Planning Model for an Analytical Review: A Feasibility Study," *Symposium on Auditing Research III,* University of Illinois, 1979, pp. 3–34.

Kask, Alex W.: "Regression and Correlation Analysis," *The CPA Journal,* October 1979, pp. 35–41.

Kendall, Maurice: *Time Series,* 2d ed., Hafner, New York, 1976.

Kinney, William R., Jr.: "ARIMA and Regression in Analytical Review: An Empirical Test," *Accounting Review,* January 1978, pp. 48–60.

———: "The Discriminatory Power of Macro Techniques in Analytical Reviews—Some Empirical Tests," *Journal of Accounting Research,* vol. 17 (supplement), 1979, pp. 148–155.

——— and Gerald L. Salamon: "The Effect of Measurement Error on Regression Results in Analytical Review," *Proceedings of the Symposium on Auditing Research III,* University of Illinois, 1979, pp. 49–64.

Lev, Baruch: "On the Use of Index Models in Analytical Reviews by Auditors," *Journal of Accounting Research,* Autumn 1980, pp. 524–550.

Makridakis, Spyros, and Robert L. Winkler: "Averages of Forecasts: Some Empirical Results," *Management Science,* September 1983, pp. 987–996.

Neter, John: "Two Case Studies on Use of Regression for Analytical Review," *Proceedings of Symposium on Audit Research,* University of Illinois, 1980.

Stringer, K. W.: "A Statistical Technique for Analytical Review," *Journal of Accounting Research* (supplement), 1975, pp. 1–13.

chapter
four

Ratio
Analysis

In the previous chapter on trend analysis we considered the use of various techniques to predict a given account balance, as a basis for evaluating the reasonableness of reported amounts. A basic limitation of this approach is that, by focusing on only a single balance, it cannot incorporate the auditor's knowledge about relationships between balances. An alternative approach, ratio analysis, is a potentially more useful approach for analytical review because it uses the auditor's knowledge of these relationships. In this manner it also facilitates the comparison of a given firm's financial position with that of other firms. Similarly, it facilitates the comparison of a firm's current performance with the record of past performance. For example, the ratio of cost of sales to sales for most firms is a very stable relationship over time and therefore is useful for evaluating current costs. Also, firms within relatively homogeneous industry groups tend to have similar ratios of this type. Thus the comparison of a firm's current cost-of-sales/sales ratio with the prior-year ratio or with an industry average ratio can often provide useful information.

The chief benefit of ratio analysis, then, is that it isolates stable (over time) or common (across firms within a given industry) relationships between account balances. Thus, it allows comparisons between firms of different sizes, since even reasonably large size differences often do not affect the relationship; that is, ratios, such as the current ratio or inventory turnover ratio, are expected to be similar for firms over a range of different sizes. Also, such relationships as the current ratio or inventory turnover are not expected to change much over time for a given firm as it grows from year to year. Again, size differences do not affect the usefulness of the ratio. The use of ratios for a given firm over time is often called "times-series analysis," and the comparison of ratios between firms at a given point in time is called "cross sectional analysis." The distinction is illustrated in Table 4-1. We discuss the uses and limitations of each in this chapter.

Table 4-1 Illustration of Financial Ratio Analysis—Time-Series and Cross-Sectional Analysis

		Current Ratio for Illustrative Firms			
		Firm A	Firm B	Firm C	Firm D	Industry Average
	1970	2.1	1.5	2.3	1.8	2.3
	1971	2.0	1.2	2.5	1.7	2.2
	1972	1.9	1.9	2.5	1.5	2.0
	1973	1.7	1.6	1.6	1.7	2.1
	1974	2.0	1.5	1.9	1.6	2.0
	1975	1.9	1.9	1.8	1.4	2.4
	1976	2.3	2.2	1.7	1.8	2.0
	1977	1.9	1.7	2.0	1.7	1.8
	1978	2.5	1.5	2.0	1.6	1.9
	1979	2.3	1.8	2.3	1.7	2.1
	1980	2.3	1.9	1.6	1.6	2.1
	1981	2.4	1.7	1.3	1.9	2.0
Cross-sectional → analysis	1982	2.2	2.0	1.5	1.8	2.1

↑
Time-series
analysis

TWO METHODS

Apart from whether a time-series or cross-sectional approach is taken, there are two methods for ratio analysis. Both are commonly used by auditors. The most well known of the two is *financial ratio analysis,* which is based on ratios between financial statement accounts, such as the current ratio or inventory turnover. Another method is to use *common-size statement analysis,* wherein each account balance is shown as a percentage of some relevant aggregate amount, such as total assets, total sales, or total expenses. The common-size statement is most often prepared in the time-series format, as in Table 4-2, but it can also be prepared in the cross-sectional format, as in Table 4-3. The time-series approach allows an analysis of changes in a firm's asset or capital structure over time, as well as a highlighting of important changes in the composition of total expenses. Alternatively, the cross-sectional approach can be used to assess how a firm's makeup of assets, capital structure, and expenses compares with that of other firms in the industry.

Note that above we have considered only ratios among financial statement accounts. Ratios of financial data to selected operating data may also be useful to the auditor. For example, the ratio of total wages to number of employees can be used to assess the reasonableness of the total wages figure. Since this latter type of analysis is best considered a form of reasonableness test, we consider it in detail in the following chapter rather than here.[1] The next section develops an approach for the auditor in using the financial ratio and common-size statement forms of ratio analysis, in both the time-series and the cross-sectional formats. This is followed by a discussion of the problems and limitations in the effective use of the analyses.

USING RATIO ANALYSIS

This section explains the application and interpretation of ratio analysis in identifying unusual relationships which signal the potential for material misstatement in a given account. Here the focus is on the analysis of individual financial statement accounts in contrast to the use of operating, leverage, and liquidity ratios to analyze the aggregate inherent risk of a client, which we covered in Chapter 2. The two techniques of ratio analysis—financial ratio analysis and common-size statements—are considered separately. Three useful references for these techniques are Leopold Bernstein's text on *Financial Statement*

Table 4-2 Sample Common-Size Statements—Time-Series Approach

DBB Company—Year Ended Dec. 31, 1983

	1980	1981	1982	1983
Common-Size Balance Sheet				
Assets				
Cash	8.2	7.8	7.5	7.8
Accounts receivable	15.1	16.1	17.2	16.8
Marketable securities	10.8	9.2	8.0	8.8
Inventories	18.1	20.9	21.2	20.7
Other current assets	5.6	5.1	4.3	4.8
Investments and other noncurrent assets	13.9	11.9	12.4	11.8
Plant and equipment	28.3	29.0	29.4	29.3
	100.0	100.0	100.0	100.0
Liabilities and equity				
Accounts payable	20.2	19.2	18.1	14.5
Other current liabilities	10.1	9.2	8.6	9.9
Long-term debt	28.6	30.0	30.8	32.4
Deferred tax	4.2	4.4	4.4	4.8
Stockholders' equity	36.9	37.2	38.1	38.4
	100.0	100.0	100.0	100.0
Common-Size Income Statement				
Revenues	97.5	97.1	95.0	96.2
Discounts and allowances	2.5	2.9	5.0	3.8
	100.0	100.0	100.0	100.0
Expenses				
Cost of goods sold	48.2	46.1	47.1	49.4
Marketing, general, and administrative expenses	11.3	18.3	16.5	12.9
Interest expense	15.1	14.8	13.2	13.0
Other expense	8.8	7.2	9.9	11.4
Tax	6.1	5.2	4.8	4.2
Income after tax	10.5	8.4	8.5	9.1
	100.0	100.0	100.0	100.0

NOTE: All figures are percentages.

Analysis (1978), George Foster's *Financial Statement Analysis* (1978), and Stewart McMullen's *Financial Statements* (1979).

Financial Ratio Analysis

The motivating feature for the use of financial ratio analysis is the utilization of relationships between account balances which the auditor

Table 4-3   Sample Common-Size Statements—Cross-Sectional
Approach

DBB Company—Year Ended Dec. 31, 1983

	Regional Competitor A	Regional Competitor B	Regional Industry Average	DBB Company
Common-Size Balance Sheet				
Assets				
Cash	5.1	8.2	6.4	7.8
Accounts receivable	15.8	20.1	17.2	16.8
Marketable securities	10.2	5.1	2.1	8.8
Inventories	22.5	21.3	24.2	20.7
Other current assets	6.1	3.4	3.3	4.8
Investments and other noncur-				
rent assets	8.0	7.9	16.3	11.8
Plant and equipment	32.3	34.0	30.5	29.3
	100.0	100.0	100.0	100.0
Liabilities and equity				
Accounts payable	21.0	21.6	17.2	14.5
Other current liabilities	8.1	12.3	10.1	9.9
Long-term debt	16.1	34.5	22.4	32.4
Deferred tax	12.5	6.4	11.2	4.8
Stockholders' equity	42.3	25.2	39.1	38.4
	100.0	100.0	100.0	100.0
Common-Size Income Statement				
Revenues	98.9	97.2	96.9	96.2
Discounts and allowances	1.1	2.8	3.1	3.8
	100.0	100.0	100.0	100.0
Expenses				
Cost of goods sold	47.3	48.1	45.4	49.4
Marketing, general, and adminis-				
trative expenses	25.8	10.9	16.0	12.9
Interest expense	7.6	14.2	8.1	13.0
Other expense	8.8	6.5	11.8	11.4
Tax	3.1	6.2	5.8	4.2
Income after tax	7.4	14.1	12.9	9.1
	100.0	100.0	100.0	100.0

NOTE: All figures are percentages.

expects to be stable over time or common across related firms or both.
For some accounts these interrelationships are clear, as they are between
the marketable securities account and the related investment income
account. But for other accounts, there are no clear interrelationships,

and therefore a financial ratio approach is inappropriate. This is the case for the cash account balance which represents the net effect of flows from several other accounts. There is no clear one-to-one relationship of cash to another account. With this in mind, we have chosen to illustrate ratio analysis for four balance sheet accounts plus selected revenue and expense accounts which have clear account interrelationships:

1. Accounts receivable
2. Inventory
3. Plant and equipment
4. Current liabilities (and unrecorded liabilities)
5. Revenue and expense accounts

The focus of the discussion is on the use of selected ratios to analyze these accounts. A comprehensive treatment of the analytical procedures for each account is presented in Chapter 6.

Accounts Receivable. The most commonly applied ratio for analyzing receivables is the receivables turnover ratio

$$\text{Accounts receivable turnover} = \frac{\text{credit sales}}{\text{average net receivables}}$$

This ratio is a good measure of a company's success in implementing a good credit policy.[2] It can be compared with prior years' results or with relevant industry ratios—the higher the ratio, the better the performance. A ratio that is low relative to prior years or to the industry average might indicate an audit problem related to uncollectibility of certain receivables. A decrease in the turnover ratio might also reflect fictitious credit sales or improper cutoff to improve profitability. Also, a lower ratio could be caused by employee fraud, if collections are not recorded properly to customer accounts. Therefore, a low ratio should be further investigated by having the client prepare a schedule for the aging of receivables, by reviewing the bad debt provisions, and by other means.

In comparing receivables turnover to the industry average, the auditor should consider differences in the nature of the production process between industries. Industries where the product is durable and has high unit value may be expected to extend credit more freely and for longer periods than industries wherein the product is nondurable and of low unit value. This would be reflected in differences in average receivables turnover for these industries.

Other ratios which might bring to light problems in receivables include:

1. *Provision for doubtful accounts* to *total receivables* or to *credit sales*. If this ratio is significantly smaller relative to prior years or the industry average, this might be an indication of an inadequate allowance for uncollectible accounts.

2. *Customer discounts* to *total receivables* or to *credit sales*. If a client has a policy of giving discounts to customers for early payment of their accounts, this ratio can be used to analyze the effect of the policy, over time and relative to the industry average. Unexpected differences here may reflect audit or management problems needing prompt attention. For example, this approach might detect fraud wherein discounts are improperly allowed by a receivables clerk in return for some consideration from the benefited customer.

3. *Largest receivable account balance* to *total receivables*. This ratio, if unusual when compared over time and with the industry average, should cause the auditor to give special attention to analyzing the validity and collectibility of this critical account.

4. *Notes receivable* to *accounts receivable*.

5. Value of *notes receivable renewed this year* to *total notes receivable*. An increase in this ratio, or in the preceding ratio, over time could reflect a collectibility problem. If the ratio is poor relative to the industry average, management attention should be directed to the problem, to reconsider current credit policy.

6. *Accounts receivable* to *current assets*.

7. *Average balance* per *customer*. A relatively high figure for this ratio, or for the preceding one, compared with prior years and the industry average could be an indication of uncollectible accounts.

Inventory. As for receivables, the most commonly used ratio for analyzing inventory is a turnover ratio.

$$\text{Inventory turnover} = \frac{\text{cost of goods sold}}{\text{average inventory}}$$

This ratio measures the relationship between inventory and sales, on the basis that a given volume of sales requires a certain level of inventory.[3] This relationship will differ across industries, and may differ owing to management policy as influenced by seasonal factors, the availability of supply, and so on. The turnover ratio can be compared over time or with the industry average. A high ratio is favorable. A high ratio might reflect more efficient inventory policies, or unrecorded inventory. A low ratio might indicate an audit problem such as obsolete or otherwise unsalable inventory, or overstated inventory valuation. For a manufacturing company, an additional turnover ratio can be computed for raw materials.

$$\frac{\text{Raw materials}}{\text{inventory turnover}} = \frac{\text{raw materials issued to production}}{\text{average raw materials inventory}}$$

The latter ratio, if relatively low, might indicate an overstocking or overvaluation of raw materials, or the presence of unusable materials inventory.

The analysis of inventory turnover can facilitate the detection of inventory theft in some cases, especially if the deviation in inventory turnover from one year to the next is due to an unusually large write-down of inventory at year-end. Inventory is normally depreciated, or written off, at year-end owing to normal circumstances of loss and waste during the year. However, an unusually large write-down in one year may simply conceal the theft of inventory in that year, or the intention of theft in the following year. Thus, either a significant improvement or a significant decline in inventory turnover could signal a potential theft.

On the other hand, the failure to make appropriate write-downs of obsolete and unsalable items could have the effect of reducing the ability of the turnover ratio to detect theft. In this case, the high inventory value, including obsolete and unsalable items, could mask shortages in the faster-moving items. Thus, consideration of inventory write-down policy and related analysis of shrinkage rates are a necessary adjunct to the proper analysis of inventory turnover.

The use of the inventory turnover ratio is subject to some important qualifications. The author should determine if the ratio is *not* comparable over time or to industry averages for any of three reasons:

1. Differences in accounting methods for valuation of inventory affect the comparability of ratios. All or some portion of inventories may be valued by different methods among firms, or may change over time for the client firm. For this reason, the turnover ratio must be interpreted carefully. Also, industry averages must be evaluated carefully. Do they reflect one method or some mix of methods for the related population of firms?
2. Firms' inventory turnover ratios differ substantially *among* industries. Significant differences in the nature of the production processes among industries lead naturally to different turnover ratios. Thus, the auditor must be confident that the client's ratio is compared with the proper industry average. For example, industries with a long production cycle will generally have high inventories and low turnovers. The book publishing and heavy equipment manufacturing industries are good illustrations. Large work-in-process inventories and long sales cycles are typical of these industries. Alternatively, industries for which the product is perishable or subject to rapid obsolescence will generally have low

inventories and high turnover. Food products and newspapers or magazines are good examples here.

3. A properly conceived and implemented management policy may dictate inventory levels different from the past or from those levels reflected in average industry turnover figures. Such factors as the availability of supply, seasonal fluctuations in demand, temporary price fluctuations, and storage costs may be involved in the management of inventory levels.

With these things in mind, the auditor can use the inventory turnover to identify the potential audit problems noted above. The turnover comparisons will be more informative if they are done by product line, and if some care is taken that the average inventory figure used in the ratio is representative of the inventory throughout the year.

Other ratios the auditor might find useful are as follows:

1. *Inventory* to *current assets*. This has the same use as the turnover ratio. When compared with prior years or the industry average, it may indicate an unexpected inventory relationship.

2. *Next year's budgeted cost of sales* to *ending inventory balance*. If available, the sales budget figures can be used to anticipate the inventory turnover for the coming year. Is this out of line with the current year's turnover ratio?

3. *Direct materials* to *total product cost*

4. *Direct labor* to *total product cost*

5. *Overhead* to *total product cost*

On either a unit cost or total manufacturing cost basis, the last three ratios can be used to analyze the composition of product costs over time and relative to the industry average. This analysis can be used to spot the improper classification of cost items, especially in the overhead component. Costs such as past service pension costs, general and administrative expense, distribution expenses, and "learning curve" costs may be improperly included in overhead.

Property, Plant, and Equipment. The most commonly used analytical procedure for depreciable asset accounts is a reasonableness test of depreciation expense, which we consider in the following chapter. The audit concern for which ratio analysis may be appropriate is the consideration of writing down some portion of underutilized assets. If the client has persistent operating problems leading to an expectation that certain assets will be indefinitely idle, the appropriate accounting treatment is to write down the assets. The ratio of net property, plant, and equipment to net sales should provide a useful measure of the firm's utilization of capacity. Compared across firms or years, if the ratio is unusually high, it may indicate a need to consider a write-down of certain assets.

Accounts Payable and Unrecorded Liabilities. A principal audit objective for accounts payable is to determine whether current liabilities are completely and properly disclosed. The two financial ratios shown below may be useful to this objective since the auditor can use these ratios to analyze the cash needs of the client. If the ratios indicate a severe cash need to support current payables, there may be a motivation for management, among other things, to understate liabilities through intentional cutoff errors or by other means. The two ratios are similar.

$$\text{Acid-test ratio} = \frac{\text{cash} + \text{marketable securities} + \text{receivables}}{\text{current liabilities}}$$

This ratio provides a measure of the immediate availability of current liquid assets to meet current liabilities.

$$\text{Defensive interval} = \frac{\text{cash} + \text{short-term marketable securities} + \text{receivables}}{\text{estimated daily cash operating expenditures (excludes depreciation)}}$$

This ratio is a measure of very short-term liquidity—how many days the most liquid assets could support the operating expenditures of the firm.

If either ratio indicates illiquidity problems, the auditor may consider the risk that the burdensome liabilities may have been understated to improve the overall appearance of the firm's financial position. Of course, critically poor ratios and severe cash needs will have alerted the auditor to audit problems in areas other than payables.

Results of Operations—Revenue and Expense. Three types of ratio analysis are commonly employed to analyze the revenue and expense accounts: (1) common-size statements, (2) the ratios of certain revenue or expense accounts to related assets accounts, and (3) the ratios of certain expense accounts to related income and expense accounts. The first of these, common-size statements, is covered in the following section, while the last two examples are presented here.

Certain expense or revenue accounts are closely related to particular asset accounts, so that the ratio of the accounts is quite meaningful and can be usefully compared over time or with that of other firms. Examples of such ratios include:

1. *Interest expense* to *debt*
2. *Interest income* to *notes receivable*
3. *Investment income* to *investments*
4. *Depreciation expense* to *gross assets subject to depreciation*
5. *Bad debt expense* to the *allowance for bad debts*
6. *Repairs and maintenance expense* to *related property, plant, and equipment*

In some cases it may be necessary to disaggregate the expense account and related asset account if, for example, it is known that certain investments have substantially different returns than others. Also, the depreciation expense ratio can be computed for major groups of assets wherein depreciation methods are the same. Apart from this, the first four ratios will generally be easy to compute and interpret. Significant deviations from the expected ratio indicate a potential accounting error.

The ratios for bad debt expense and repair and maintenance expense may not be as easily interpreted, however. These relationships are to a significant extent discretionary in nature. Though the ratios should display a predictable long-run pattern (e.g., bad debt expense might be computed as a percent of credit sales), the ratio may fluctuate in any one period because of differences in management's policies for that period. This is particularly true for maintenance expenses which can be postponed without immediate breakdowns or loss of productivity. The auditor should interpret an unexpected deviation for either of these two ratios with these considerations in mind.

Another type of ratio useful for analyzing the expense accounts is the ratio of certain expenses to related income or expense amounts, for example:

1. *Payroll taxes* to *payroll expense*
2. *Employee benefit expense* to *payroll expense*
3. *Income tax* to *income before tax*

These ratios should have a stable, predictable pattern, especially for the first two. Any significant deviation, if not reflecting a change in tax rates or management benefits policy, would signal the potential for accounting error of some kind. The income tax ratio is less easily interpreted since it may not be comparable over time because of changes in tax law or because of the tax effects of nonrecurring decisions, such as an unusually large charitable donation in a given year.

Common-Size Statements

Common-size statements are often prepared for both the balance sheet accounts and the income statement accounts. However, the analysis of the income statement accounts tends to be far more useful than does analysis of the balance sheet since most revenue and expense accounts bear some relationship to total sales, whereas a breakdown of the composition of total assets or total equities is generally less meaningful. For one thing, the balance sheet accounts may include nonoperating items which will reduce the comparability of the common-size percentages, both over time and across firms. Additionally, an analysis of the composition of total assets, liabilities, and equities has value primarily in assessing inherent risk, as we have discussed in Chapter 2, rather than in identifying the potential for error in a given account, as is our subject in this chapter.

The special value of common-size analysis of revenue and expense accounts is that most of the individual accounts bear some relationship to the aggregate—total sales. As sales increase, most expense items increase in a predictable way, and thus the comparison of the common-size percentages over time or across firms can be very meaningful. To illustrate, we discuss the analysis of the common-size percentages for the following four income statement accounts. Other revenue and expense accounts can be analyzed in a similar fashion.

1. Sales returns and discounts
2. Cost of goods sold
3. Selling expense
4. Research and development expenses

The accounts for *sales returns* and *discounts on sales* bear a natural relationship to total sales. Any significant deviation of this percentage, over time within the firm or when compared across firms, provides an indication of potential error in the accounting for these items. For example, a steep increase in the rate of sales returns might be an indication of obsolete or unsalable inventory.

The ratio of *cost of goods sold* to *sales* is among the most common of the ratios used by auditors. For most firms this ratio has a very stable and predictable pattern which makes it very useful for comparison across time or with similar firms. It is most useful when computed by product line since the components of cost and profit margins can vary significantly for different products, and changes in product mix can affect the aggregate rates. In some cases the ratio is used in its equivalent, inverse form, the ratio of gross margin to total sales. The two are interpreted in a similar manner. A significant and unexpected deviation in the ratio for any product line, unless explained by changes in price or productivity, could indicate a lack of consistency in accounting for inventory or in treating a certain component of cost. A cost item might be improperly included in or excluded from product cost, for example.[4]

The cost-of-goods-sold ratio was instrumental in detecting fraud in one case wherein cash payments on receivables were taken by a receivables clerk. This left the detail list of customer balances less than the general ledger, but the bookkeeper, thinking the differences were immaterial, made a balancing entry to debit sales and credit receivables. This was done several times through the year, and by year-end, sales were so understated that the cost of sales ratio was significantly increased. Upon investigating the increase, the auditor detected the defalcation.

The ratio of *selling expense* to *sales* should also represent a stable and predictable relationship. To the extent that selling expenses are directly proportional to sales, as for a sales representative's commissions, the ratio is easily interpreted. However, to the extent that some components of selling expense are not related to sales, as for sales representatives' salaries, the ratio has little meaning. Thus the proper interpretation of this ratio, *as for those of most expense accounts,* requires an understanding of the nature of the underlying cost behavior—is it strictly variable (with sales revenue), strictly fixed, or a mix. The usefulness of the analysis of the ratio, then, is directly proportional to the extent to which the expense item is *strictly variable* in nature. Also, some portion of selling expense might be discretionary, as for nonrecurring special promotion efforts. Items of this nature will also distort the comparability of the ratio to that for prior years.

The ratio of *research and development expenses* to *sales* can provide a useful basis for an analysis of the accounting for ongoing research efforts. However, its interpretation is subject to the same limitations identified above—the distortion due to fixed costs and nonrecurring items. Additionally, research and development expenses are a type of expense wherein judgment must be employed to determine what portion of current expenditures is capitalized. *FASB Statement 2,* "Accounting for Research and Development Costs," has limited the bounds for this judgment considerably, but many uncertainties remain as to the proper accounting for these costs. Thus, the analysis of this ratio for a stable and ongoing research effort could be used to signal any change in management's accounting policy for certain of these costs.

PROBLEMS AND LIMITATIONS IN USING RATIO ANALYSIS

We have just seen that it is very important to know whether a cost item is strictly variable or not when analyzing it through common-size statements. This is one example of many of the problems and limitations in using ratio analysis. These can be conveniently grouped into the following three categories:

1. The effect of different accounting conventions
2. The assumed nature of the relationship underlying the ratio
3. The determination of what is a significant deviation

These three problem areas are relevant for all types of ratio analysis, though different accounting conventions affect intra-industry comparisons far more than they do time-series comparisons. These problems, along with problems in using industry data, are presented later in the chapter, together with some suggestions for using these data most effectively.

Effect of Accounting Conventions

A primary reason why ratios may be noncomparable over time or across firms is the use of different accounting conventions. There are two types of accounting conventions involved, and there may be differences in either: (1) the manner in which the ratio is computed and (2) the accounting policy for recognition and valuation for the related financial statement accounts.

As Gibson and Boyer (1980) point out, there is a general lack of uniformity in the manner in which the ratios are computed—what is included in the numerator and in the denominator of the ratio. For example, they point out that two of the principal sources of industry ratios compute inventory turnover in a different manner. Robert Morris Associates uses the ratio of cost of sales to inventory, where *Dun's Review* presents net sales to inventory. The latter gives a higher turnover ratio. The auditor must be alert for such differences in using ratio analysis. Additionally, when average ratio figures from trade or industry publications are used, care must be taken that the ratios for each sampled firm were computed in the same manner.

The second type of accounting convention relates to accounting policies which may differ across firms or over time. We list some of the more important potential differences below.

1. Inventory valuation—LIFO, FIFO, etc.
2. Differences in management conservatism in making certain accounting estimates such as the allowance for doubtful accounts or the adjustment for obsolete and unsalable inventory
3. Differences in the cost accounting methods used, the allocation of overhead, and the treatment of variances

It is clear that consistency for both types of accounting conventions is likely to be greater for a given firm over time than for a comparison across firms or with industry averages. Thus, the auditor must be particularly alert for this kind of problem when comparing a firm's ratios to industry data.

The Assumed Nature of the Relationship Underlying the Ratio

For a ratio analysis to be meaningful we must be satisfied that the relationship between the numerator and denominator is (1) strictly variable, (2) strictly linear, (3) complete, and (4) stable over time and consistent across firms. Rarely are these assumptions met perfectly in practice, but often they are satisfied sufficiently for the ratio analysis to be meaningful.[5] Consider each assumption.

The Relationship Is Strictly Variable. It is convenient in illustrating this assumption to use certain labels, as follows:

$$R \text{ (the ratio)} = \frac{N \text{ (the numerator)}}{D \text{ (the denominator)}}$$

For example, the ratio of selling expense to sales (R) would be the result of selling expense (N) divided by the sales (D). We start with a very general description of the relationship between sales and selling expense

$$\text{Selling expense} = \text{function of sales}$$

If we assume the relationship is linear, the general linear model with labels would be

$$N = A + RD$$

where A is the intercept of the linear equation. It corresponds to the fixed cost portion of the total selling cost (N) while RD is the total variable cost portion. Thus, the assumption of a strictly linear relationship means that A equals zero, and $R = N/D$. If, however, A is not zero and there is fixed cost, then $R = N/D - A/D$, wherein the last term (A/D) represents bias. Now the ratio R is not comparable for different levels of D because of the bias term. More simply, N/D in this case represents unit variable cost which should be constant for a range of values for D, but A/D will vary with changes in D thus causing the bias.

In summary, the auditor must understand the nature of the relationship between the numerator and denominator of the ratio under analysis, particularly for the ratios of expense to sales involved in common-size income statements. When the fixed component A is present, the comparison among ratios must be interpreted carefully. The auditor can use the cost accounting concept of a *relevant range* to assist when the fixed component is present. That is, the comparability of the ratios is directly proportional to the size of the difference in the denominator for the ratios compared. For example, given the ratios R_1 and R_2, where $R_1 = N_1/D_1$ and $R_2 = N_2/D_2$, if D_1 and D_2 are relatively close, then the comparison of the ratios can be meaningful.

In our studies of auditor judgment we conducted an experiment to investigate the ability of unaided auditors to apply an understanding of this assumption when interpreting common-size income statements. Only 7 of the 29 auditors differentiated a ratio where the intercept A was present from one where the relationship was strictly variable. This suggests that some auditors may not sufficiently understand the importance of this assumption when using ratio analysis.

The Relationship Is Strictly Linear.   We have just seen that the analysis of ratios is based on the special case of the general simple linear model with an intercept A equal to zero. It follows then that we are assuming a linear relationship between the numerator and denominator. This assumption is reasonable for many expense categories, especially if we apply the concept of the relevant range. For example, selling expense which is primarily composed of a sales representative's commission of 15 percent would have an approximately linear relationship with sales. On the other hand, if the commission rate increases or decreases with an increase in sales for the individual sales representative, the relationship is actually nonlinear.

Another example of a nonlinear relationship is the inventory turnover ratio for a firm which employs the economic order quantity (EOQ) formula for optimizing production runs or purchase order size. The simple EOQ model is as follows:

$$EOQ = \sqrt{\frac{2 \times \text{annual sales} \times \text{purchase order cost}}{\text{storage cost}}}$$

As can be seen from the formula, average inventory (approximately EOQ/2) is directly related to the *square root* of sales rather than sales per se. Thus, the inventory turnover ratio does not reflect a linear relationship, and turnover rates for different levels of sales will not be comparable.

As for the "strictly variable" cost assumption above, a response to the problems related to the linearity assumption is to apply the concept of the relevant range. Thus, if the differences in the denominators of the ratios being compared are not significantly different, the ratios will be reasonably comparable.

The Relationship Is Complete. The assumption we address here is that the denominator of the ratio *alone* and no other item of financial or operating data influences the numerator. Consider again the example of the ratio of selling expense to sales. Suppose the relationship between selling expense and sales is best expressed by

Selling expense = function of (sales, sales mix, . . .)

That is, selling expense is now assumed to be influenced by two or more variables, in this case by sales, sales mix, and perhaps other variables. Then the general linear model should be of the following form, where D_1 represents sales, and D_2 represents sales mix (assume A equals zero):

$$N = R_1D_1 + R_2D_2$$

Then, the selling-expense-to-sales ratio is biased by the additional variable in the equation:

$$R_1 = \frac{N}{D_1} - \underbrace{\frac{R_2D_2}{D_1}}_{\text{Bias}}$$

The practical result of this is that two selling expense ratios may not be comparable because of differences in sales mix. Unfortunately, the auditor rarely has enough knowledge of the nature of the relationships affecting the numerator of a ratio to assess the potential for this type of bias. The application of multivariate statistical methods, such as multiple regression analysis, can be used to identify these multiple relationships, but these techniques may be cost-effective on only the largest audit engagements.

The Relationship Is Stable over Time and Consistent across Firms. This is perhaps the most obvious of the assumptions of the nature of the relationship expressed by the ratio. It relates to the nature of the operating and financial structure of the firm. For example, the installation of a computer-based inventory management system should have a significant effect on average inventories. Inventory turnover ratios before and after the development would not be comparable. The same can be said for differences in financial and operating structure across firms.

Determining What Is a Significant Deviation

A basic limitation of the effective use of ratio analysis is the lack of useful guidance in determining a cutoff or threshold for identifying significant deviations. This is largely a matter of auditor judgment, based on knowledge of the client's operations, the quality of the client's controls, and other factors. Our studies of auditor judgment suggest that, without prompting, auditors use a cutoff of somewhere between 5 and 10 percent of the amount of the ratio, for common-size statement analysis. The thresholds for balance sheet ratios are probably higher, though these were not included in our study.

USING INDUSTRY DATA

This section points out the difficulties in using industry figures for comparison with a firm's ratios. An approach for most effectively using industry data is presented. This approach uses the auditor's knowledge of the client's business to construct a specialized industry index for the client.

The Difficulties

Some of the problems in using industry data have already been explained. In Chapter 2 we discussed the problems in using industry leverage, liquidity, and operating ratios in analyzing the financial risk component of inherent risk. And earlier in this chapter we listed some of the accounting conventions which can differ across firms so that the affected ratios are not comparable. Now we consider three additional problems in using the industry data.

First, it is difficult to define an industry. Most definitions are based on the nature of the end product such as "furniture and fixtures" or "paper and allied products." The SIC code to the two-digit level of aggregation is widely accepted. However, many analysts would admit that very often a company does not "fit" well within the group because of unique product diversification, vertical or horizontal integration, and so on.

A second and related problem in using industry comparisons is the numerous possibilities for natural differences between firms within well-defined industry categories. For example, firms in the same industry may differ substantially in financial or operating factors, and in related ratios, for the following reasons:

1. Geographic separation, differences in price levels and costs of operations.
2. Different ownership or financial structure. For example, the levels of current assets may be significantly different for an independently run firm than for a subsidiary of a conglomerate firm.

3. Nonoperating factors in the balance sheet or income statement.
4. Different levels of capacity utilization.
5. Product diversification.
6. Age and productivity of assets.
7. Different customer mix, number of customers, and geographic dispersion including international clientele.

This is merely a partial listing. The auditor who has a good understanding of the client's business will be able to identify those unique aspects of the business which might distinguish it from others in the industry.

These potential intra-industry differences are reflected in intra-industry variability of ratios. For example, Trapnell (1977) found that many ratios did not consistently differentiate between two-digit, SIC-code industry groups; that is, there was approximately as much interindustry variability in ratios as there was intra-industry variability. However, the best differentiating ratios were those related to certain of the asset accounts, such as the current ratio and the asset turnover ratio. In a related study, Gupta and Huefner (1972) had results consistent with the above. The consequence of the high intra-industry variability is that an industry average ratio does not provide a very reliable target.

The comparison of firm to industry ratios is laden with the difficulties identified above. In many cases, the auditor will be satisfied that they are not too severe for the engagement at hand and that the tie-in to industry data is meaningful and useful. Exhibit 2 at the end of the chapter provides a listing of selected industry ratios. Exhibit 3 then lists many sources of industry data which are available.

Developing Your Own Industry Index

Rather than use available industry figures, the auditor may choose to develop his or her own index, in such a way as to avoid many of the problems discussed above. This may only be cost-effective on the larger audit engagements.

To implement this approach, the audit firm would obtain access to one of the available computer-based sources of company data, such as the *COMPUSTAT* file, available from Standard & Poor's Corporation. The *COMPUSTAT* file contains financial statement data and certain operating data for approximately 2000 companies, for both quarterly and annual periods. The database is updated throughout the year, so it should be sufficiently current for most audit purposes. Also, though not perfectly reliable, large databases of this type have been found to be reasonably accurate and to be among the most accurate sources of data available for research or analysis.

Having obtained the database, the auditor's next step is to develop the programming necessary to access the database and to present the desired analysis in a usable manner. An interactive programming approach would be most desirable because of the timeliness of this approach and because it permits the auditor to address "what if" questions to the database and obtain an immediate response.

The purpose of the programming is twofold. First, it must facilitate the auditor's task of identifying and aggregating firms which are comparable to the audit client. This can be done in a sequence of interactive question and answer steps wherein the program asks the auditor to specify certain pertinent facts about the client such as product mix, total sales, and geographical dispersion. On the basis of these facts, the program searches the entire database for comparable firms. The search process can be fine-tuned by adding instructions concerning how many comparable firms are desired, which facts are most important in the search process, etc. The result of this phase of the programming is a pool of comparable firms.

The second purpose and second phase of the programming is to produce the desired ratio analysis from the pool of comparable firms. Again, an interactive question and answer approach can be used to elicit the desired ratios and method of presentation. A critical question at this step is how the ratios of the firms in the pool are to be aggregated—by the simple average, the median, or what. The problem here is that most (80 to 90 percent) of the distributions of financial ratios (across firms) are not symmetrical. Generally, the distribution has a peak at the left and long tail to the right; that is, most firms have a small value for the ratio, but a significant minority have relatively large values. In this situation, the simple average of the ratios is not representative of that for a majority of the firms in the pool. Four approaches are used to aggregate ratios for firms in the pool.

1. Simple Average.   Very often this is used, but for reasons cited above, it is most often not a representative number.

2. Median.   This is the ratio which evenly splits the pool (50 percent are larger and 50 percent smaller). It is generally smaller than the mean and more representative of the pool. The median is used in the published statistics of Dun and Bradstreet's *Key Business Ratios* and in Robert Morris Associates's *Annual Statement Studies*. This is the approach we favor.

3. Value-Weighted Aggregate.   The aggregate can be computed as the weighted average across the firms, wherein the weighting factor is total assets, sales, earnings, common equity, or a similar financial statement aggregate. This approach produces an aggregate which is most heavily influenced by the larger companies. The approach is used in practice, but the auditor should question whether it makes sense for a given audit client. Is the client very large or small, and how would this affect the comparison?

4. Data Transforms. An approach which is used by some researchers is to transform the data, typically using the log transform, so that the resulting distribution of ratios is more nearly symmetrical. The aggregate ratio is then compared with the transformed ratio for the audit client. This approach requires that all data be positive, but this is not often a problem with the ratios we have discussed. Using a transform has an effect similar to that of using a median: it produces a smaller aggregate. It differs from the median in that it takes into account the value of each ratio in the pool.

One final matter regarding the aggregation of ratios is that the auditor should have a planned approach for dealing with two occasional problems. One is the case wherein certain data items are missing for a given firm in the pool. Should that firm be deleted from the pool for all computations, or only for computations involving that item? Also, what approach is taken when one or more of the firms in the pool have ratios which are *very much* different from the ratios for the other firms? Such firms are called "outliers."[6] There is no standard methodology for handling outliers. Some argue that outliers should be deleted from the pool. Others argue that if a single, large (or small) outlier is removed, the smallest (or largest) data item should also be removed, and so on, until all outliers are removed. Other methods may also be used. The important thing is for the auditor to have developed a plan for treating outliers before accessing the database, so that the analysis is done in an objective and consistent manner.

Assistance in developing the database and programming can come from many sources. The auditor may have the expertise within the firm, as do many auditing firms. Alternatively, the auditor can look to the many computer software vendors, such as those cited in Chapter 3, or to the following time-sharing vendors:

COMSHARE, Inc.
  Compass Services
  1114 Avenue of the Americas
  New York, NY 10036
  (212) 398-6800

Scientific Time Sharing Corporation
2115 East Jefferson
Rockville, MD 20852
(301) 984-5000

General Electric Corporation
Information Services
1221 Avenue of the Americas
New York, NY 10020
(212) 997-0358

Another good source is the experienced consultant.

FOOTNOTES

[1]When operating data are in either the numerator or the denominator of the ratio, we consider this to be a reasonableness test rather than ratio analysis. This does not distinguish the two techniques perfectly, since there are examples where the ratio of two financial statement accounts is computed as part of a reasonableness test (e.g., interest expense to liabilities; interest income to investments). However, we find it generally true that reasonableness tests employ operating data, whereas "ratio analysis" is typically understood to mean the ratios between financial statement accounts. In a sense, reasonableness tests may be considered a subset of the more general approach, ratio analysis, and we could have treated the two approaches together in this chapter. But the application and interpretation of the two are sufficiently different that we have chosen to cover them in separate chapters.

[2]The "average collection period," 365 days divided by the receivables turnover ratio, is also in common use. The collection period provides the same information in a different format, and is interpreted in the same manner as the turnover ratio. The auditor may use either, but since they are redundant, there is no need to calculate both.

[3]The "number of days sales in inventory," 365 days divided by the inventory turnover ratio, is an alternative and equivalent ratio in terms of both the information provided and the manner of interpretation.

[4]A detailed statement accounting for variations in cost of goods sold and gross margin is illustrated in Bernstein (1978, pp. 587–90).

[5]A complete, rigorous presentation of the material covered in this section can be found in Lev and Sunder (1979).

[6]By common technical definition, an "outlier" is an item which lies more than 3 or 4 standard deviations away from the mean of the other data items.

REFERENCES

Beaver, W. H., P. Kettler, and M. Scholes: "The Association between Market-Determined and Accounting-Determined Risk Measures," *Accounting Review*, October 1970, pp. 654–682.

Bernstein, Leopold A.: *Financial Statement Analysis*, rev. ed., Irwin, Homewood, Ill., 1978.

Deakin, E. B.: "Distributions of Financial Accounting Ratios: Some Empirical Evidence," *Accounting Review*, January 1979, pp. 90–96.

Foster, George: *Financial Statement Analysis*, Prentice-Hall, Englewood Cliffs, N.J., 1978.

Gibson, Charles H., and Patricia A. Boyer: "The Need for Disclosure of Uniform Financial Ratios," *Journal of Accountancy*, May 1980, pp. 78–84.

Gonedes, N. J.: "Evidence on the Information Content of Accounting Numbers: Accounting-Based and Market-Based Estimates of Systematic Risk," *Journal of Financial and Quantitative Analysis*, June 1973, pp. 407–444.

Gupta, M. C., and R. J. Huefner: "A Cluster Analysis of Financial Ratios and Industry Characteristics," *Journal of Accounting Research*, Spring 1972, pp. 77–95.

Horrigan, James O. (ed.): *Financial Ratio Analysis: An Historical Perspective*, Arno, New York, 1978.

Lev, Baruch, and Shyam Sunder: "Methodological Issues in the Use of Financial Ratios," *Journal of Accounting and Economics*, 1979, pp. 187–210.

McMullen, Stewart Yarwood: *Financial Statements: Form, Analysis and Interpretation*, 7th ed., Irwin, Homewood, Ill., 1979.

Trapnell, Jerry Eugene: "An Empirical Study of the Descriptive Nature of Financial Ratios Relative to Industry Operating Characteristics," unpublished Ph.D. thesis, University of Georgia, Athens, 1977.

EXHIBIT 2

COMPARATIVE SELECTED INDUSTRY RATIOS

The ratios presented here are the median values for the period 1978 to 1981. The industry category listing is that used by Bavishi et al. The types of ratios presented include all those identified in Table 2-2 for which we could obtain stable figures for the 1978–1981 period. Industry ratios which were not stable during the period were excluded, and this excluded all the operating ratios and a few of the leverage ratios shown in Table 2-2. The ratios presented in this exhibit were stable throughout the 4-year period.

Industry Category	Leverage Ratios			Liquidity Ratios			
	Long-Term Debt to Total Capitalization	Total Debt to Total Assets	Total Debt to Equity	Current Ratio	Quick (Acid-Test) Ratio	Accounts Receivable Turnover	Inventory Turnover
Food and beverages	0.28	0.47	1.2	1.8	0.9	11.4	7.6
Metal manufacturing	0.30	0.45	1.1	2.1	1.0	7.0	6.2
Mining and petroleum	0.28	0.44	1.0	1.4	0.9	8.7	10.1
Textiles and apparel	0.25	0.43	1.2	2.8	1.3	6.3	4.9
Tobacco	0.31	0.50	1.0	2.0	0.6	12.2	4.6
Paper, fiber, and wood	0.28	0.40	0.9	2.0	1.0	9.1	7.9
Publishing	0.20	0.36	0.7	1.6	1.0	6.1	11.4
Chemicals	0.28	0.43	1.0	2.1	1.1	6.1	6.3
Rubber, plastic products	0.35	0.50	1.3	2.0	1.0	6.5	6.1
Glass, concrete, abrasives	0.25	0.40	0.8	2.0	1.1	7.4	7.3
Electronics, appliances	0.23	0.48	1.1	2.0	1.0	6.1	5.2
Transportation equipment	0.40	0.56	1.6	1.8	0.8	8.1	6.1
Photo and scientific equipment	0.14	0.36	0.6	2.6	1.3	4.9	4.1
Automotive	0.25	0.48	1.0	2.0	0.8	8.1	5.6
Aerospace	0.22	0.51	1.5	1.8	0.7	9.1	4.1
Pharmaceuticals	0.14	0.37	0.7	2.3	1.2	5.4	4.6
Cosmetics, soaps	0.20	0.40	0.8	2.2	1.2	6.6	5.6
Office and computing equipment	0.21	0.43	0.9	2.0	1.0	4.3	4.1
Industrial and farm equipment	0.24	0.45	1.0	2.3	1.0	5.9	4.1
Musical instruments	0.32	0.50	1.1	2.4	1.0	5.6	4.7

SOURCES: Adapted from V. B. Bavishi, F. D. S. Choi, H. A. Shawky, J. P. Sapy-Mazella, *Analyzing Financial Ratios of the World's 1000 Leading Industrial Corporations,* Business International Corp., New York 1981; Leo Troy, *Almanac of Business and Financial Ratios,* Prentice-Hall, Englewood Cliffs, N.J. (annual).

EXHIBIT 3

SOURCES OF INFORMATION ON INDUSTRY RATIOS

Professional and commercial sources

Dun and Bradstreet, Inc., Business Economics Division.

Key business ratios. Important operating and financial ratios in 71 manufacturing lines, 32 wholesale lines, and 22 retail lines and published in *Dun's Review* of modern industry. Five-year summaries are also published. The data are presented in three ranges: lower quartile, median, and upper quartile.

Cost-of-doing-business series. Typical operating ratios for 185 lines of business, showing national averages. They represent a percentage of business receipts reported by a representative sample of the total of all federal tax returns.

Moody's Investor Service.

Moody's manuals contain financial and operating ratios on individual companies covered.

National Cash Register Company.

Expenses in Retail Businesses. Biennial. Operating ratios for 36 lines of retail business, as taken from trade associations and other sources including many from *Barometer of Small Business.*

Robert Morris Associates.

Annual Statement Studies. Financial and operating ratios for about 300 lines of business—manufacturers, wholesalers, retailers, services, and contractors—based on information obtained from member banks of RMA. Data are broken down by company size. Part 4 gives "Additional Profit and Loss Data."

Standard & Poor's Corporation.

Industry surveys in two parts: (1) basic analysis and (2) current analysis; contain many industry and individual company ratios.

Almanac of Business and Industrial Financial Ratios by Leo Troy, Prentice-Hall, Inc., Englewood Cliffs, N.J.

A compilation of corporate performance ratios (operating and financial). The significance of these ratios is explained. All industries are covered in the study; each industry is subdivided by asset size.

The Federal Government

Small Business Administration.

Publications containing industry statistics:

Small Marketers Aids.
Small Business Management Series.
Business Service Bulletins.

U.S. Department of Commerce.

Census of Business—surveys wholesale trade and releases summary statistics; monthly wholesale trade report; ratios of operating expenses to sales.

U.S. Department of the Treasury.

Statistics of income, corporation income tax returns. Operating statistics based on income tax returns.

Federal Trade Commission.

Quarterly financial report for manufacturing, mining, and trade corporations. Contains operating ratios and balance sheet ratios as well as the balance sheet in ratio format.

Sources of Specific Industry Ratios

Federal Deposit Insurance Corporation *Bank Operating Statistics*. Annual.

Institute of Real Estate Management. Experience Exchange Committee. *A Statistical Compilation and Analysis of Actual Income and Expenses Experienced in Apartment, Condominium and Cooperative Building Operation*. Annual.

Discount Merchandiser. *The True Look of the Discount Industry*. June issue each year. Includes operating ratios.

Eli Lilly and Company. *The Lilly Digest*. Annual.

National Electrical Contractors Association. *Operation Overhead*. Annual.

National Farm & Power Equipment Dealers Association. *Cost of Doing Business Study*. Annual.

Journal of Commercial Bank Lending. "Analysis of Year End Composite Ratios of Instalment Sales Finance and Small Loan Companies."

Harris, Kerr, Forster & Company. *Trends in the Hotel-Motel Business*. Annual.

Ohio Lumber and Building Product Dealers Association. *Survey of Operating Profits*. Compiled by Battelle and Battelle. Annual.

American Meat Institute. *Financial Facts about the Meat Packing Industry*. Includes operating ratios.

Chase Manhattan Bank. *Financial Analysis of a Group of Petroleum Companies*. Annual.

National Office Products Association. *Survey of Operating Results of NOPA Dealers*. Annual.

American Paint and Wallcoverings Dealers. *Report on Annual Survey*.

Printing Industries of America. *Ratios for Use of Printing Management*. Annual.

Laventhol Krekstein Horwath & Horwath. *Restaurants, Country Clubs, City Clubs: Reports on Operations*. Annual.

National Association of Textile and Apparel Wholesalers. *Performance Analysis of NATAW Members*. Annual.

Bibliographies

Robert Morris Associates, *Sources of Composite Financial Data—A Bibliography, 3d ed., N.Y., 1971, 28 pages.* An annotated list of sources, with an index, by specific industry, at front.

Sanzo, Richard, *Ratio Analysis for Small Business,* 3d ed., U.S. Small Business Administration, Small Business Management Series, no. 20, 1970, 65 pages. "Sources of Ratio Studies," pp. 22–35, lists the industries covered by basic sources such as D&B, Robert Morris Associates. Also includes the names of trade associations which have published ratio studies. Published financial and operating ratios are also occasionally listed in the monthly *Marketing Information Guide.*

SOURCE: Adapted from Bernstein (1978), pp. 83–85.

chapter
five

The
Reasonableness
Test

I went home, and to bed, three or four hours after midnight. . . . An accidental sudden noise waked me about six in the morning, when I was surprised to find my room filled with light. . . . Rubbing my eyes, I perceived the light came in at the windows. I got up and looked out to see what might be the occasion of it, when I saw the sun just rising above the horizon, from whence he poured his rays plentifully into my chamber.

This event has given rise in my mind to several serious and important reflections. I considered that, if I had not been awakened so early in the morning, I should have slept six hours longer by the light of the sun, and in exchange have lived six hours the following night by candlelight; and, the latter being as much more expensive light than the former, my love of economy induced me to muster up what little arithmetic I was master of, and to make some calculations, which I shall give you, after observing that utility is in my opinion, the test of value. . . .

In the six months between the 20th of March and the 20th of September, there are

Nights 183

Hours of each night in which we burn candles 7

Multiplication gives for the total number of hours 1,281

These 1,281 hours multiplied by 100,000 the number of
    inhabitants (of Paris) give 128,100,000

One hundred twenty-eight millions and one hundred
    thousand hours, spent at Paris by candlelight, which, at
    half a pound of wax and tallow per hour, gives the
    weight of 64,050,000

Sixty-four millions and fifty thousand of pounds, which,
    estimating the whole at the medium price of thirty sols
    the pound, makes the sum of ninety-six millions and
    seventy-five thousand *livres tournois* 96,075,000

An immense sum! that the city of Paris might save every year, by the
economy of using sunshine instead of candles.

Benjamin Franklin
"An Economical Project"
(apparently written Mar. 20, 1784)

Benjamin Franklin appears to have been one of the earliest advocates of
daylight saving time. His frugal disposition and keen intellect which led
to this advocacy are well illustrated in this series of multiplications which
projects immense savings for the city of Paris. These computations are
characteristic of what we describe in this chapter, the reasonableness
test. The reasonableness test is generally a very simple computation or
series of computations which develops an estimate of an amount
through the use of relevant financial and operating data. A good
example is the estimation of bad debt expense from current sales and
receivables data, or the estimation of payroll expense from data about
the number of employees, average wage rate, and time worked.

    Since the reasonableness test employs a limited amount of data and
simple computations, the resulting estimate is generally viewed as a good
approximation, but not as precise an estimate as would be obtained, say,
from statistical methods. But, since the reasonableness test requires far
less auditor time, it may often be more cost-beneficial than other
estimation methods.

    An important aspect of the use of a reasonableness test in audit
planning is that it requires the auditor to consider all the financial and
operating factors (independent variables) which are relevant for the
amount to be estimated (dependent variables). That is, to complete a
reasonableness test the auditor must in effect develop a simple model to
explain changes in the dependent variable by analyzing changes in
related independent variables. We touched on this type of modeling

approach briefly in Chapter 3 in connection with trend analysis. However, the focus of Chapter 3 was changes over time, a time-series analysis using a time-series model. In contrast, we extend that idea in this chapter to the simple one-period model which the auditor can analyze with pencil and paper. The important thing here is that the reasonableness test requires the auditor to structure, or "model," the process of developing the desired estimate.

The benefits of modeling the estimation process are the greater knowledge acquired by the auditor and the greater precision of the estimate. Both benefits stem from the explicit recognition of the relevant independent variables and from the quantification of the relationships between these variables that is required to complete the reasonableness test. To illustrate, let us consider the hypothetical case of an auditor involved in planning year-end tests for payroll expense. The auditor performs trend analyis and observes a 9 to 10 percent increase over the previous year. Having noted that this rate of increase is consistent with the approximately 10 percent rate of inflation in the local economy, and with the 8 to 12 percent average wage increases, the auditor gains confidence that a modest level of substantive testing is required. In contrast, if the auditor had taken a reasonableness test approach, he or she would have found (in this hypothetical case) that the company had had to interrupt production and lay off plant personnel for an entire month to repair a crucial piece of equipment. The cost of repairs was improperly charged to direct labor expense so that payroll expense is overstated and repairs expense is understated. The reasonableness test would have required an analysis of hours worked and in this way would have led the auditor to detect the accounting classification error.

The chapter is organized as follows: First, there is a discussion of the reasonableness test method for both the single- and the multiple-independent-variable cases. This includes illustrative applications for selected accounts. Second, there is a brief presentation of the manner in which a statistical approach or an expected value approach could be used to enhance the precision of the reasonableness test.

REASONABLENESS TEST METHODS

The auditor performing a reasonableness test to analyze an account balance begins with a simple model of financial and operating factors affecting that account. Four different modeling approaches are possible, as illustrated in Table 5-1. Each of the four model types represents a different approach to the reasonableness test.

Table 5-1   Four Types of Models of the Account Balance

What the Model Predicts (dependent variable)	Complexity of the Model	
	One Independent Variable	Two or More Independent Variables
Current account balance	Type one	Type three
Change in account balance from prior year	Type two	Type four

The models differ according to what it is the auditor is predicting with the reasonableness test (the dependent variable is either the account balance or the change in the account balance) and according to the number of financial and operating factors (independent variables) the auditor plans to incorporate in the model. Assuming all the independent variables are relevant, the greater the number of independent variables, the more informative is the model and therefore the more precise its prediction. Of course, the multiple-variable model is also more complex and costly to apply than the single-variable model.

The auditor chooses also whether to apply a model which predicts the total current account balance, or the change in balance from the prior year. While the former is more common and perhaps more intuitively appealing, the latter may be more economical and effective in those situations wherein the prior year's balance is audited. The reason for this is that, by considering only the change in the balance, the auditor is able to eliminate from the model all those independent variables which did not change from the prior year. These variables would therefore be irrelevant for the *change* model, whereas they would probably have to be included in the *current-balance* model. Thus, in this case the change model is simpler, and more effective and economical.

One-Variable Models (type one and type two)

The most popular model for use in reasonableness tests appears to be the type one model. There are many examples of this approach in accounting and auditing. It is widely used as an estimating technique in a variety of contexts. For example, construction costs are often predicted on the basis of square feet of livable space. Also, factory overhead costs are often predicted as an amount per direct labor hour. And, revenues from hospital room charges for a given period can be estimated directly from room charge and occupancy data.

These simple estimates can be computed quite easily and are often reasonably accurate. Many times they are just as accurate as detailed methods that are more time-consuming and costly. It is often argued that the simple, one-variable models are as useful as the more complex models because those variables not included will generally have offsetting effects, so that on the average, the use of the single most important independent variable produces very good results. This is likely to be one of the reasons for the wide usage of the simple methods in practice.

The reader is referred back to those two sections of Chapter 4 which dealt with the use of ratios to analyze revenue and expense accounts, and to the use of common-size income statements. Both of these forms of analysis are closely related to the type one reasonableness test model. Both analyses use a simple relationship between accounts to predict an account balance. For example, a reasonableness test of the account *repairs and maintenance expense* could be done by examining the ratio of repairs and maintenance expense to the value of the related plant and equipment. Similarly, the ratio of a sales representative's commission expense to sales could be used to examine the reasonableness of this expense category.

In contrast to the above illustrations, reasonableness tests typically involve a selected operating datum as the independent variable—occupancy rate, production level, and the like. That is, the reasonableness test examines the correspondence that should exist between the operating and financial data. Quite naturally, there should be good correspondence between operating data and the "results of operations" portion of the financial data. In contrast, there is less reason to expect a relationship between operating levels and the levels of the "stock" balances of the financial statements—assets, liabilities, and equities. Thus, reasonableness tests are naturally more applicable for revenue and expense accounts, the financial record of results of operations.

For some organizations virtually every revenue and expense account can be readily tied to an index of operating activity. For example, room charge revenue for hospitals and hotels should be easily correlated to occupancy rates. Revenue for freight haulers can be related to tons of material carried. Similarly, utilities expenses, fuel costs, and related production costs are easily estimated from data about production activity.

For other organizations, the direct correspondence between operating data and financial results may not exist, or reliable operating data may not be available. For example, sales levels for retailers often cannot be tied to a readily available, independent index of operating activity. This would probably be the case for a videotape and phonograph record retailer. A convenient predictor variable is not available in this case. Certain demographic and macroeconomic data may be useful in predicting broad movements of videotape and record sales, but not with the precision required by auditors. Thus, a reasonableness test approach is not applicable in this situation.

Because it is most common, the type one reasonableness test model has been the focus of our discussion to this point. The type two modeling approach is very similar. For example, the auditor examining hotel revenue may have good reason to assume that the occupancy rate for the current year is very nearly the same as for the prior years, but room charges have increased by an average of 10 percent. Then, an appropriate reasonableness test would be to predict current year's revenue as 110 percent of the prior-year (audited) amount.

Index Models

A very special and unique single-variable approach for the type one reasonableness test is the use of an index model.[1] Index models are useful particularly for large manufacturing companies, where a variety of different sizes of products of a similar design are made. For example, the manufacture of products such as furniture, steel and concrete pipes, electric motors, certain appliances, and fuel tanks represents a situation where the index model could be applied. Basically, the index model is an exponential equation which predicts the cost of a given size of a product on the basis of the known size and cost of a product of similar design. Index models therefore can be used to test the reasonableness of inventory costs in cases where production output varies in size but is similar in type. The index model is

$$C = C_r \left(\frac{Q_c}{Q_r} \right)^m$$

where C = total cost sought for design size Q_c

   C_r = known cost for a reference design size Q_r

   Q_c = design size

   Q_r = reference design size

   m = correlating exponent, $0 \leq m \leq 1$ $m = 1.0$ means no economies of scale in production

The use of the model can be illustrated as follows. Suppose the auditee manufactures concrete tanks of similar design in many different sizes, lengths, and diameters. Assume the value of $m = 0.6$ for tanks ranging from 100 to 1000 cubic feet of capacity. The value for m may be known from engineering studies or analyses of past cost records. Assume also that it is known that a tank of 200 cubic feet has a cost of $2500, and assume that the auditor wants to assess the reasonableness of the cost of a batch of 600-cubic-foot tanks, as reported by the client. The 600-cubic-foot tanks are a new product for the firm, and the auditor is not familiar with the cost behavior of the larger tanks, so the index model analysis is desired. The estimated cost of each tank of the 600-cubic-foot size is

$$C = 2500\left(\frac{600}{200}\right)^{0.6} = \$2500 \times 1.933182 = \$4832.96$$

If the exponent m is reliable, then a good estimate of the larger tank is approximately $5000, as computed above. The size of the tank increases threefold, whereas the cost nearly doubles.

This illustration is for the model in the basic form, and it may require adjustment for price changes, if the price of the "reference" size is dated. Also, the determination of the exponent m should take into account any technological differences, batch size differences, or other factors which might impact the comparability of the costs for the two product sizes involved. Tables of values of m for a variety of products can be found in engineering reference books such as the text by Peters and Timmerhaus (1968).

Multiple-Independent-Variable Models

In many cases the auditor may find that two or more independent variables are necessary to estimate the given account balance with acceptable precision. For example, consider again the case of estimating room charge revenue for a motel or hotel on the basis of occupancy and room charge data. This is the simple one-variable problem discussed earlier. If, however, the motel or hotel has a seasonal rate structure, then it will be necessary to add the seasonality dimension as a second independent variable. Now, the estimated revenue is computed for each rate season, and the seasonal figures are aggregated to obtain the desired estimate for the annual amount.

Two additional examples will further illustrate this multiple-variable approach. The first example involves the reasonableness test of the fuel expense for the auto and truck fleet of a large construction firm. This is an example of the type three model in that it involves the estimation of an account balance without the use of the prior year's balance. The example is outlined in worksheet form in Table 5-2. Two types of fuel, eleven types of vehicles with related fuel consumption measures, and usage figures for each vehicle type are incorporated in the analysis. Much of the information required for the analysis is readily available from the financial records (fuel cost per gallon, number of vehicles of each type). The fuel consumption data could be obtained by inquiry of management and corroborated by an outside source such as the local dealer for the vehicle. The usage data may be available in the client's

Table 5-2 Reasonableness Test Worksheet

Fuel Expense for Hypothetical Construction Company

No.	Vehicle	Fuel Consumption	Usage (and Data Source)	Gallons Used	Total Fuel Used	Fuel Cost
			Gas*			
59	Small autos	20 mpg	$21,000 \times 59 = 1,239,000$ miles (no client records; estimated mileage from samples of 10 autos)	61,950		
23	Large autos	10 mpg	$24,000 \times 23 = 552,000$ miles (no client records; estimated mileage from sample of 6 autos)	55,200		
44	Pickup trucks	8 mpg	836,241 miles (client records)	104,530		
36	Vans	7 mpg	333,036 miles (client records)	47,576	269,256	$282,719
			Diesel†			
6	Flatbed trucks	4 mpg	39,204 miles (client records)	9,801		
4	Dump trucks	3 mpg	29,280 miles (client records)	9,760		
2	Payloaders	3 gal/h	3152 hours (client records)	9,456		
3	Bulldozers	3 gal/h	$\frac{3152}{2} \times 3 = 4728$ hours (no records; assumed same as for payloader)	14,184		
1	Gooseneck trailer	2 gal/h	16,380 hours (client records)	8,190		
2	Graders	2 gal/h	190 working days (client records) $190 \times 8 \times 2 = 3040$ hours	6,080		
2	Scrapers	2 gal/h	Assumed same as for grader	6,080	63,551	$ 62,280
			Estimated total fuel expense			$344,999

*Cost = $1.05 per gallon.
†Cost = $0.98 per gallon.

operating reports or maintenance records. The hypothetical data given in Table 5-2 reflect the reasonable assumption that this type of data is available for some vehicles and not for others. Where the usage data are not available, the auditor must provide an estimate. This can be done by taking a sample of the vehicles of a given type, obtaining the records or data necessary to figure the usage for these vehicles, and then projecting the sample results to the total number of vehicles. Alternatively, the auditor can use rough estimation methods based on whatever relevant information is available. For example, a usage estimate could be based upon the known number of working days in the year together with some assumption of the radius (in miles) of the region in which the operations took place.

Once the relevant data are assembled, as in the hypothetical case just depicted, the estimate of aggregate fuel expense is easily derived. This can be compared with the recorded amount for reasonableness. If the difference is significant, the auditor, depending on the materiality of the amount, may choose to do further testing or propose an adjustment to fuel inventory and fuel expense. Since fuel inventory for a construction company may be in small amounts in many locations, an accurate year-end inventory measurement with acceptable cutoff may be impractical. In this situation both the client and the auditor may feel that a reasonableness test in the manner described is an appropriate approach for adjusting fuel inventory and fuel expense accounts for the current year-end statements. A similar case could be made for taking this approach in similar circumstances for the accounts, supplies inventory, and supplies expense.

A second example illustrates the type four model, wherein the prior year's account balance is included in the model for estimating the current year's balance. The payroll expense account provides a useful illustration. The three steps of the analysis for a hypothetical case are shown in Table 5-3. The analysis begins with the prior-year amount. Then, the three elements involved in explaining a change in the balance over the current year are presented and analyzed. The three elements are (1) the wage rate, (2) the number of employees, and (3) the number of hours worked per employee. If the change in wage rate or the number of hours worked for the current year differs significantly for certain subgroups of employees, then these groups would be separately analyzed. However, often wage increases are across the board, and merit increases affect all employee groups, so that the use of a plantwide change in wage rate is often reasonable. Also, changes in the number of hours worked generally affect all employee groups, and the plantwide analysis is reasonable in this case.

In the hypothetical illustration we have assumed that wages increased

Table 5-3   Reasonableness Test Worksheet
Hypothetical Payroll Expense Account

1. Wage expense for the prior year (audited) $2,962,430
2. Elements affecting change in wage expense (and data for
    current year)
    a. Increase (decrease) in average wage rate applicable
        to these personnel (8% increase effective midyear;
        net effect is 4% annual increase, or *104%*)   1.04
    b. Increase (decrease) in the number of applicable
        personnel (loss of 4 of 151 positions, effective near
        the middle of the year)

$$\frac{151 - (4 \times 1/2)}{151} = \frac{149}{151}$$ 0.9868

    c. Increase (decrease) in the number of hours worked
        for applicable personnel (additional 40 h/employee
        of overtime, early in the year)

$$(1/52)(1.5)$$ 0.02884

3. Estimated wage expense for current year

    $2,962,430 [(1.04) × (0.9868) + 0.02884] $3,125,695

---

on the average by 8 percent over the prior year and that the increase was effective near the middle of the year. Also, there was a loss of two full-year-equivalent personnel from the prior-year total of 151. Finally, the entire applicable work force worked the same number of normal hours as the prior year, but worked approximately 40 hours of overtime compared with none in the prior year.

As the third step of the worksheet shows, these three elements are combined using simple arithmetic to obtain an estimate for the current-year payroll expense. Notice that the wage rate factor (1.04) and the percentage change in number of personnel (.9868) are multiplicatively related since they apply to the entire year. The effect of the change in the number of overtime hours, however, is additively related to the prior-year amount since it occurred early in the year and thus was not affected by the other two elements. Our work with auditors performing analytical review tasks such as this shows that auditors often fail to assess correctly whether a relationship is multiplicative or additive, as in this example. The tendency appears to be to assume an additive relationship, even when it is not appropriate. An awareness of this bias should help auditors to mitigate its effect on their own judgments.

Another common practice we have observed among auditors is the extensive use of rounding of figures in reasonableness tests such as the

Dependent Variables	Independent Variables
Sales or sales returns and allowances	Competition Interest rates Demographic trends Employment trends Economic indicators Advertising policies Pricing policies
Cost of sales	Inflation rate Fuel costs Labor rates Materials costs and availability Union contracts Production technology Personnel policies Employee benefit policies Location of facilities
General, selling, and administrative expenses	Employment and space rental contracts Number of sales personnel

above illustrations. The effect of this rounding is to reduce the precision of the prediction, since fewer significant digits are used. Auditors should be aware of this tendency toward rounding and understand its effect on the precision of their predictions.

To summarize, the reasonableness test approach can be characterized as the method which involves (1) identifying the relevant variables, (2) identifying the proper (multiplicative or additive) relationship between the variables, and (3) combining the variables to obtain an estimate of the current account balance. It follows that effective use of the model requires a good understanding of the operating environment of the client. This is necessary so that the relevant independent variables are properly identified. Also, it is important for the auditor to have the analytical ability to identify the correct form of the relationship between variables, whether multiplicative, additive, or some combination. This latter ability probably improves with audit experience, though many would also argue that some auditors are inherently better able to identify these relationships correctly than are others. Research from diverse areas of judgment investigation provides little guidance as to whether experience, ability, task context, or some other factor may be associated with the occurrence of these judgment errors. However, the research does consistently show that both expert and novice decision makers commonly make judgment mistakes of this type.

The examples we have shown are illustrative of the wide variety of contexts in which a reasonableness test approach can be useful. Because the approach typically models the relationship between financial results and operating data, the revenue and expense accounts will be naturally more amenable to the analysis. The table on the preceding page is offered as a partial listing for use in identifying the relevant independent variables when developing a reasonableness test.

STATISTICAL METHODS

A way to enhance the precision of the reasonableness test approach is to apply statistical methods or probabilistic models. These methods add precision because they (1) quantify the uncertainty present in the estimation problems and (2) provide a means for evaluating the accuracy of the estimate.

The most appropriate statistical method in this context is regression analysis which was described briefly in Chapter 3. The technical aspects of this method are presented in Appendix 4. The application of regression analysis provides a more precise predictive model because it utilizes available data to produce a best-fitting linear model. The quantitative measure of predictive accuracy is the *standard error of the estimate,* which is provided with the regression results. It is a range around the predicted value wherein the auditor can be fairly confident the unknown "true" value will lie.

Regression can be used in either a time-series or cross-sectional model. In the time-series approach the auditor collects data on the account balance and related operating data for the most recent 10 to 40 periods, usually months. The model which results from the data provides a prediction for the current balance based on the current operating data. As an example, the auditor could develop a time-series model for wage expense, using the independent variables identified in the example in the previous section.

Wage expense = average hourly wage rate
$\times$ average number of employees
$\times$ average hours worked per employee

In symbols

$$W = WR \times E \times H$$

Note that this model is *not* linear since the independent variables are multiplied rather than added. Thus, a linear regression on these data would be inappropriate. Rather, the auditor would have to transform the data to an equivalent linear form. The logarithmic transform is most common; when applied to a multiplicative relationship, the resulting model is linear:

$$\log W = \log WR + \log E + \log H$$

The auditor transforms each data item by taking its logarithm (most computer-based statistical packages will do this automatically). The resulting equation is in log form, so that the desired estimate for wage expense is found by taking the antilog of the amount predicted by the equation.

The log transform is a convenient approach for dealing with nonlinear relationships in regression models. As noted before, the auditor must be alert to determine properly whether a multiplicative (nonlinear) or additive relationship applies for the model under analysis. Once this has been ascertained, it will be clear whether or not a log transform is necessary.

Another type of regression approach is to develop the model from cross-sectional data. For example, a regression equation to estimate sales revenue for different locations of a chain of auto repair shops would require a cross-sectional model. All the data would be obtained from the current period. The relevant independent variables might be staff size, inventory value, square feet of repair service area, and so on. In this case the model is fitted from data across different stores in the chain, rather than across time as for the wage expense example.

THE EXPECTED VALUE METHOD

Alternatively, if time and resources are such that regression analysis is not cost-effective, the auditor can apply probability modeling to obtain a measure of the accuracy of the estimate from the model. The probability modeling approach centers on the use of subjectively assessed probabilities for the independent variables. The approach is simple to apply and requires little time. The probabilities reflect the auditor's knowledge of both the range within which the independent variable lies and a likelihood for where it is most likely to fall within that range, usually near the midpoint. Though there are many ways to obtain subjective probabilities, one of the most convenient is based on the beta probability distribution that is often used for network scheduling models. To use this method the auditor simply estimates three values—the most likely value *(M)* for the independent variable, the smallest possible value *(S)* for the independent variable, and the largest possible value *(L)*. Then, the best prediction for the variable (called the "expected value," or "*EV*") may be found by

$$EV = \frac{S + 4M + L}{6}$$

And, the measure of the accuracy of the prediction is inversely proportional to the statistical variance *(VAR)* of the probability distribution for the variable, which is given by

$$VAR = \frac{(L-S)^2}{6}$$

The square root of *VAR* is called the "standard deviation" of the probability distribution, and it is interpreted in the same manner as the "standard error of the estimate" in the regression context. That is, it gives a range (plus and minus) around the expected value such that the auditor can be fairly confident that the unknown true value of the distribution will lie in that range. See Appendix 4 for a more complete discussion of the proper interpretation of the standard error of the estimate.

As an example of this approach, consider again the wage expense case. And suppose the auditor is uncertain about the number of hours worked per employee *(H)* because of inadequate records or for other reasons. But the auditor is confident that the figure is between 35 and 45 hours per week and is most likely to be 38 hours per week. Then using our probability model we can obtain the expected value and variance as follows:

$$EV_H = \frac{35 + (4)(38) + 45}{6} = 38.67 \text{ hours}$$

$$VAR_H = \frac{(45 - 35)^2}{6} = \frac{100}{6} = 16.67 \text{ hours}$$

This information can be used to evaluate the precision of the estimate for wage expense in the following manner. Suppose that, in addition to the above *EV* and *VAR* for the number of hours per employee *(H)*, we know that the applicable average wage rate *(WR)* is $8.50 per hour and that the number of employees *(E)* is 150. Then *weekly* wage expense is estimated as

$$\text{Wage expense per week} = WR \times W \times E$$
$$= \$8.50 \times 38.67 \times 150$$
$$= \$49,304.25$$

$$\text{Annual wage expense} = \$49,304.25 \times 52$$
$$= \$2,563,821$$

We now utilize the variance $(VAR = 16.67)$ to obtain the range around the estimated amount wherein we would expect the true value to lie. This range is approximately $270,000 for the above data.[2] This interval is the computed standard deviation for wage expense and can be interpreted as a measure of the accuracy of the estimate. This clearly reflects a very imprecise estimate, as the interval is quite large relative to the estimated amount. The reason for this is the lack of precision in the estimate for the number of hours (H), which we have allowed to range from 35 to 45 hours, a very wide range in itself. A more precise estimate for H would have produced a correspondingly more precise estimate for the annual wage expense. For example, suppose that, as above, the auditor's best guess for the number of hours H was 38, but in contrast to the above, the auditor was confident that the number of hours would be between 38 and 42. Now, recomputing the expected value and variance

$$EV_H = \frac{38 + (38)(4) + 42}{6} = 38.67 \text{ hours}$$

$$VAR_H = \frac{(42 - 38)^2}{6} = \frac{16}{6} = 2.67 \text{ hours}$$

Notice that EV_H does not change, so the estimated annual wage expense will also remain the same as for the previous case, at $2,563,821. But now the confidence range for the estimate is much smaller, at approximately $108,000.

The above probability model is easy to use and interpret and does not require complex calculations. The auditor can use it as a shorthand, preliminary method to assess the precision of a given estimate. The regression method and more detailed analysis can provide a more complete evaluation of the precision of the estimate, if necessary.

FOOTNOTES

[1]This section on index models is adapted from Ostwald (1974), pp. 201–202. The index model is also sometimes called the "power law and sizing model."

[2]The precision interval is found by computing the standard deviation of wage expense as follows: $VAR_W = (WR \cdot E \cdot 52)^2 VAR_H$, and the standard deviation is $\sqrt{VAR_W}$. For $VAR_H = 16.67$ the standard deviation is $270,695, and for $VAR_H = 2.67$ it is $108,335. Note that while the standard deviation computed for this example can be interpreted as a measure of accuracy, as for the standard error of the estimate in the regression model, it does not provide a basis for constructing a symmetric precision interval around the estimate unless the underlying distribution is symmetric. When the smallest (S), largest (L) and midpoint

(M) values for the distribution are such that M is equidistant from S and L, the distribution is symmetric and the precision interval is symmetric. When M is not equidistant from L and S, the distribution is not symmetric and, therefore, a symmetric precision interval cannot be constructed.

REFERENCES

The Complete Works of Benjamin Franklin, vol. VI, John Bigelow (ed.), Putnam, New York, 1888, pp. 277–283.

Ostwald, Phillip F.: *Cost Estimating for Engineering and Management,* Prentice-Hall, Englewood Cliffs, N.J., 1974.

Peters, Max S., and Klaus Timmerhaus: *Plant Design and Economics for Chemical Engineers,* 2d ed., McGraw-Hill, New York, 1968.

chapter
six

Using Analytical Review for Selected Accounts

This chapter ties together much of the material in various parts of the book. Whereas previous chapters have dealt primarily with the description of a variety of analytical review procedures and selected illustrative applications, the objective of the present chapter is to present a somewhat comprehensive approach for selecting the extent and type of analytical review to apply when analyzing a given account. The material is presented in two steps. First, there is a general discussion which develops an approach for determining when and to what extent to apply a trend analysis, ratio analysis, or reasonableness test method when analyzing balance sheet accounts or revenue and expense accounts. The discussion, which is based in part on research results, shows that the potential effectiveness of each of the three methods differs somewhat in either context. While balance sheet accounts are best analyzed by ratio analysis, the revenue and expense accounts are best examined by either ratio analysis or a reasonableness test. Trend analysis is useful to a lesser degree in both cases. The arguments and research which support these generalizations are developed in this first section of the chapter.

Second, we present a suggested listing of analytical review methods for selected financial statement accounts, together with a brief explanation of the methods and their interpretation. The seven accounts included in this section are as follows:

1. Accounts receivable
2. Inventory
3. Property, plant, and equipment
4. Accounts payable, unrecorded liabilities, and other liabilities
5. Revenue accounts
6. Expense accounts
7. Prepaid expenses; accrued liabilities

The last three of these—revenue, expense, and prepaid expenses and accruals—are groups of accounts. These accounts are treated as groups for economy in presentation since the applicable methods are the same within each group. Some accounts are excluded from the presentation because they are generally not effectively analyzed by analytical review methods. An account may not be amenable to analytical review for either of the following two reasons, or for a combination of the two:

1. The account balance is very much subject to management discretion and does not for this reason show a predictable relationship with other financial or operating data. The cash account, investments, long-term assets, and long-term liabilities are accounts which are of this nature.
2. The account is influenced by many complex factors which are not likely to remain constant over time. Tax expense is one such account.

The third and final section of the chapter deals with the situation wherein analytical review is used to allocate audit effort within the context of a single account balance. For example, the audit of inventory for a chain of retail stores involves the determination of which subset of all retail outlets will be selected for inventory test procedures. This decision is based in part on the materiality of the inventory amount of each location and upon the auditor's evaluation of risk at each location. Analytical review methods can be used to supplement this decision process by helping to determine which outlets should be examined, using as a basis for the decision any unusual relationships of financial and operating data for the outlet. Four of these methods are described in this final section of the chapter.

A GENERAL APPROACH FOR USING ANALYTICAL REVIEW

To develop a general approach, or strategy, for using analytical review, we consider the issues of the proper timing, extent, and nature of analytical review for both balance sheet and income statement accounts.

Timing of Analytical Review

Analytical review is applicable at three phases of the audit engagement—planning, field work, and final review. Should there be differences regarding which of the three methods—ratio, trend, or reasonableness test—are applicable at each phase? Probably there is no difference since each of the methods is easy to apply and each generally requires a limited amount of data and computation. Also the objective for each of the three phases is relevant for each balance sheet and income statement account. Thus, the auditor will find each method to be applicable at each phase and for each account.

One exception to this might be that a reasonableness test would be infeasible at the planning phase because, at this early point in the engagement, certain of the relevant operating data may not be available to the auditor. Also, it is likely that in the final review phases the reviewing auditor will principally use the less quantitative of the methods, ratio and trend analysis, to get a quick "over the top" look at the reasonableness of the statements. Apart from these exceptions, it seems that timing is not an important factor in developing a strategy for choosing an effective analytical review approach for a given account.

Extent of Analytical Review

Again, since each of the three types of analytical review methods generally requires little time to perform, the issue of "extent of testing" is not really applicable to the analytical review itself. Rather, the issue over the extent of testing revolves around how much evidence is obtained through the analytical review to reduce the extent of subsequent substantive testing. This is the "work-reducing" role of analytical review as set forth in professional standards. In determining the extent to which subsequent testing can or cannot be reduced, the auditor considers four important aspects of the analytical review method, the account under analysis and the results of applying the method:

1. *Risk.* The auditor evaluates the potential for material error to occur in the account and not be detected by existing controls.

2. *Materiality.* The auditor assesses the impact on the financial statements taken as a whole if the account balance is substantially misstated. This is the concept of account materiality.

3. *Precision.* The auditor evaluates the precision associated with the use of the analytical review method for the account. That is, how much confidence can the auditor have in the projections and results of the method? For example, the gross margin percentage is often considered a relatively precise form of analytical review since the cost-of-sales/sales relationship is generally a very stable, predictable relationship. On the other hand, the ratio of maintenance expense to total sales is generally less stable and predictable, and thus in our terms, it provides less precision.

4. *Results.* If the results of the analytical review indicate no unusual or unexpected relationships for the account, then the auditor may be able to reduce the scope of subsequent substantive testing if he or she is satisfied as to risk, materiality, and precision for the account.

The auditor considers all four of these factors in choosing the scope of subsequent testing. At one extreme, if risk and materiality are low and precision is high, and if the results show nothing unexpected, then this evidence argues for the auditor to reduce the scope of subsequent tests. The extent of the reduction should vary proportionately to the degree that the four factors indicate the absence of material error. Alternatively, if all four factors are unfavorable, then the auditor may consider increasing the scope of substantive testing beyond the current plan. There is not now a mathematical formula which relates the four factors to a precise amount or percentage of reduction (or increase) in scope; this is left to the auditor's judgment. What is important is that the auditor give sufficient consideration to each factor.

Of the four factors, risk, materiality, and results relate directly to the account being examined, whereas precision is affected both by the nature of the analytical review method and by the account under examination. That is, certain methods are more precise than others, and some accounts are more easily analyzed than others, thereby leading to more precise results. Examples of relatively simple and relatively complex accounts were given directly above. Also, the reader may refer again to the section of Chapter 3 which deals with the evaluation of prediction error. Here there is a discussion of the nature of the confidence interval around the prediction, that is, the potential for error associated with different methods. For example, because of the precision derived from statistical methods, the use of regression-based analytical review methods is generally more precise than other methods. Also, a reasonableness test may be more precise than other methods since it can capture the relationship between operating and financial data and thereby explain a greater portion of the behavior of the account than would be obtained, say, from a simple trend analysis.

One final comment about the four factors. They are to be interpreted as independent elements of the decision problem; that is, the degree or level for any one of the factors should not influence the evaluation of any other factor. For example, the fact that the results were unfavorable (detected unexpected relationships) should not influence the auditor's evaluation of the precision associated with the analytical review method. If it does, the auditor's decision is improperly biased. This point should be noted carefully, because we have observed in our research a tendency for auditors to perceive incorrectly that certain of these factors are not independent.

Nature of Analytical Review

In developing a strategy for using analytical review, the auditor considers three available methods—trend analysis, ratio analysis, and the reasonableness test. Choosing from among these methods depends in part on the desired precision, as noted above. Also, certain methods are generally more effective for certain accounts, as summarized in Table 6-1. Three important patterns emerge from this table. The first is that

Table 6-1   Usage of Analytical Review Methods

| | Method | | |
Type of Account	Trend Analysis	Ratio Analysis	Reasonableness Test
Balance sheet account	Of limited usefulness*	Useful	Of limited usefulness
Revenue and expense account	Useful	Very useful	Very useful

*The term "useful" is meant to indicate the relative cost-benefit and precision of the method.

analytical review tends to be more useful (effective and precise) for the income statement accounts than for the balance sheet accounts. The reason for this is that the income statement accounts reflect "flows" (receipts, purchases, disbursements), whereas the balance sheet accounts represent "stocks" which are the net effect of one or more different flows. Thus, the balance sheet accounts are inherently more complex and therefore less easily analyzed by simple analytical review techniques. Kaplan (1979b, 1980) has studied the time-series behavior of balance sheet and income statement accounts and found the balance sheet accounts to be more difficult to "model," or predict. The best models of the balance sheet accounts were those that attempted to capture the flows in the accounts, as you would expect, but even these more complex models were inferior in predictive ability to those for the income statement accounts. The auditor can infer from this that analytical review applications for the balance sheet accounts may not be as effective and precise as desired.

A second pattern that emerges from Table 6-1 is that the income statement accounts are most effectively analyzed by ratio analysis and reasonableness tests. Here, ratio analysis refers to the ratio of a revenue or expense account to (1) an asset or liability account, (2) another expense account, or (3) total sales. The last ratio is commonly called the "common-size" income statement. The reason ratio analysis and reasonableness tests should be more effective and precise than trend analysis is that they are more likely to capture the variations in operating activity (the flows) which influence these account balances. In this sense, ratio analysis and reasonableness tests are more "informative." Trend analysis, in contrast, only captures the change from the prior year, and this change is made up of the net effect of many different factors, or flows.

The third and final pattern seen in Table 6-1 is that, when one is analyzing balance sheet accounts, ratio analysis is preferred. The reason is based partly on the observed success in the practical use of turnover ratios. Also, because balance sheet accounts reflect stocks rather than flows, the otherwise strong reasonableness test method is inappropriate since it captures operating (flow) relationships.

These three patterns are reasonably descriptive of the overall approach auditors appear to be using, so far as is indicated by our limited survey of audit practice. The one exception is that auditors in practice tend to use trend analysis somewhat more extensively than is suggested by our analysis above. Other results of our survey are that, as you might expect, the extent, timing, and nature of the usage of analytical review do not differ significantly for audits in the range of 500 to 2500 budgeted hours. For the largest engagements (2500 hours and larger), there was a greater tendency to use specialized analytical review methods in certain areas, especially inventory, but overall the pattern was one wherein the usage of analytical review appeared not to be influenced by engagement size. Also, as expected, there were no differences in usage that could be explained by either the ownership of the client (private or public) or the geographic location of the client.

SUGGESTED ANALYTICAL REVIEW FOR SELECTED ACCOUNTS

The objective to this point in the chapter has been to help the auditor develop an effective overall approach for using analytical review. We now show a suggested list of specific procedures to use in applying this overall approach for each of seven selected accounts—accounts receivable, inventory, long-term assets and depreciation, accounts payable and other liabilities, revenue accounts, expense accounts, prepaid expenses and accrued liabilities.

In using the suggested lists, the auditor should keep in mind the overall strategy plus the five following matters:

1. What is the audit objective for the analytical review? Is the audit question the completeness, existence, ownership, collectibility, valuation, cutoff, or proper classification for the account under analysis? Stating an objective is very important. We have found that there is a tendency for auditors to perform unnecessary analytical review, in part because it is viewed as an inexpensive audit procedure. If the auditor cannot state a specific objective for the analytical review, then it probably is not worthwhile.

2. One method which is useful for identifying the potential for material error is simply to review the adjustment summary from the prior year's working papers. An adjustment in the prior year is a useful signal of the likelihood of need for an adjustment in the current year.

3. Many of the "indicators" of risk which were identified in Chapter 2 should be kept in mind as the auditor approaches a specific audit area. For example, turnover of key personnel and other operating problems should influence the potential for accounting error. This and item 2 above are reminders that an analytical review procedure is only one of the sources of information the auditor can use to detect areas with high potential for material misstatement.

4. Whenever possible, the analytical review results should be summarized for each account and maintained on a permanent working paper. This will facilitate the auditor's comparison of ratios and other data with data of prior years.

5. Whenever feasible, the analytical review should be performed on a divisional or product line level so as to facilitate the detection of unusual and unexpected relationships.

Accounts Receivable

As we will see, most analytical review procedures for accounts receivable address the audit objective of assessing collectibility of accounts receivable. The procedures also provide some evidence for evaluating completeness and existence. The listing below is intended to be comprehensive; thus, the auditor may choose to apply only a portion of these for any given audit engagement. The relevance of each will vary with the circumstances.

The procedures are listed in five groups which address four different audit issues and one "other" category.

1. *Collectibility of receivables*
   a. Receivables turnover, the ratio of credit sales to average net receivables
   b. Average balance per customer
   c. Ratio of accounts receivable to current assets
   d. Notes receivable to accounts receivable
   e. Renewed notes receivable to notes receivable
   f. Aging schedule of accounts receivable
2. *Provision for doubtful accounts*
   a. Ratio of provision for doubtful accounts to credit sales
3. *Discount policy*
   a. Ratio of customer discounts to credit sales
4. *Special problems*
   a. Ratio of largest receivable account balance to total receivables
   b. Analysis of receivables for related parties
   c. Analysis of any significant year-end fluctuations in credit sales
5. *Other*
   a. Roll-forward of beginning balance *plus* credit sales *less* cash receipts to estimate the ending balance of accounts receivable

The use and interpretation of these procedures need little explanation. Most of them are commonly used in auditing practice. All the procedures emphasizing ratios are described briefly in Chapter 4. Chapter 4 also has a useful discussion of the problems and limitations involved in ratio analysis.

Table 6-2 illustrates a worksheet that can be used to summarize the information derived from applying the procedures in a hypothetical case. The worksheet would become a part of the permanent work papers for the audit engagement in order to facilitate year-to-year comparisons of the ratios and results of procedures. Significant trends and year-to-year changes would be easily detected in this manner. Also, to be most useful, the worksheet should be prepared for each major distinguishable operating segment of the auditee since the relationships analyzed by these ratios and other procedures are likely to differ across segments.

The last three procedures listed above will generally require some working paper support which would include the relevant calculations, the auditor's explanation of the source and credibility of the data, and the auditor's conclusion for the analysis. The conclusion is brought forward to the permanent worksheet, and a working paper (W/P) reference is made for the detailed analysis. Note that the permanent worksheet also contains space for the auditor to show any other significant factors which are important in evaluating the potential for material error in the account, such as the turnover of key personnel in the receivables area.

Inventory

As for accounts receivable, analytical review is useful for achieving certain audit objectives when examining inventory, but not useful for other objectives. We present a suggested listing of procedures for each audit objective in examining inventory, and we take a worksheet approach to aggregating the information, very much as was done for receivables.

Analytical review's principal contribution is to assist the auditor in testing inventory pricing, and in efforts to detect misclassification errors arising from improper treatment of overhead. The latter might occur from improperly including a cost (maintenance expense, employee travel, etc.) in overhead.

A secondary contribution of analytical review is to examine for obsolete inventory, improper handling of inventory shrinkage, and improper cutoff. Analytical review can contribute little, unfortunately, to the audit objectives of examining existence and ownership. These objectives are achieved by other substantive procedures.

The analytical review procedures recommended for inventory are as follows, listed by audit objective:

1. *Pricing, Obsolescence, and Shrinkage*
   a. Turnover ratio, the ratio of cost of sales to average inventory.
   b. Gross profit percentage.
   c. Raw materials turnover, the ratio of raw materials issued to production versus the average raw materials inventory.

Table 6-2 Accounts Receivable—Hypothetical Analytical Review Worksheet

Analytical Review Procedure	1980	1981	1982	1983
Part 1: Collectibility of Receivables				
Turnover ratio	10.8	11.6	9.9	10.5
Average balance per customer	$252	$310	$288	$301
Ratio of accounts receivable to current assets	62%	58%	60%	65%
Notes receivable to accounts receivable	15%	12%	14%	16%
Renewed notes receivable to notes receivable	0%	15%	18%	9%
Aging, %				
0–30 days	63	59	60	54
30–60 days	15	10	16	18
60–90 days	11	16	15	14
Over 90 days	11	15	9	14
Part 2: Provision for Doubtful Accounts				
Ratio of provision for doubtful accounts to credit sales	2.5%	3.1%	2.4%	2.2%
Basis for provision	Specific + 2% of credit sales	Specific + 2% of credit sales	Specific + 2% of credit sales	Specific + 2% of credit sales
Part 3: Discount Policy				
Ratio of customer discounts to credit sales	0.8%	1.1%	0.5%	0.4%
Credit terms	2%/10; net 30	2%/10; net 30	2%/10; net 30	2%/10; net 30

Part 4: Special Problems

	2.1%	5.4%	3.6%	4.8%
Ratio of largest receivable account balance to total receivables				
Analysis of receivables for related parties	OK Not OK W/P ___	OK Not OK W/P ___	OK Not OK W/P ___	OK Not OK W/P ___
Analysis of any significant year-end fluctuations in credit sales	OK Not OK W/P ___	OK Not OK W/P ___	OK Not OK W/P ___	OK Not OK W/P ___

Part 5: Other

Roll-forward of beginning balance *plus* credit sales *less* cash receipts (should approximately equal ending balance)	OK Not OK W/P ___	OK Not OK W/P ___	OK Not OK W/P ___	OK Not OK W/P ___
A material adjustment in the account this year?	Yes No W/P ___	Yes No W/P ___	Yes No W/P ___	Yes No W/P ___
Other significant factors, such as turnover of key personnel?	Yes No W/P ___	Yes No W/P ___	Yes No W/P ___	Yes No W/P ___

d. Shrinkage ratio, the ratio of inventory write-downs to total inventory.

e. Analysis of standard cost budget variances; review of standard costs for reasonableness.

f. Reasonableness test using average prices and units on hand to estimate the current inventory value.

2. *Misclassification and Cutoff*

a. Comparison of the ending balance of products for sale to budgeted sales.

b. Comparison of the ending balance of raw materials to budgeted usage.

c. Examination of the relationship between materials, labor, and overhead to total product cost.

3. *Other*

a. Inspection for unusually large purchases near year-end.

b. Roll-forward of beginning balance *plus* purchases *less* cost of sales. Should approximately equal ending balance.

The above procedures should be completed for each major group of related products, or on a product line basis, if feasible. Notice that some of the procedures apply to materials inventory as well as to the inventory of products for sale. The use and interpretation of these procedures are well known. For example, an unexpectedly low turnover ratio indicates a potential for a significant amount of obsolete inventory or overstated valuation. Chapter 4 has a discussion of some problems and limitations in using many of these procedures.

Table 6-3 illustrates a worksheet approach for analytical review of inventory based upon the above procedures. It is a permanent worksheet so that significant trends and changes over the years can be more readily detected. Also, some of the procedures require additional working paper support to document more extensive analysis. For example, a schedule of purchases near year-end can be used to identify any unusually large purchases which might indicate an attempt to artificially improve the financial statements.

Property, Plant, and Equipment

Because of relatively infrequent transactions in this account, it is often most cost-effective to audit it by detail methods. However, analytical review can be useful for two audit objectives for this account. One objective is to test the accuracy of the allowance for depreciation and related current expense. This can be done by a reasonableness test in which assets are grouped into reasonably homogeneous groups for lives and depreciation methods. Depreciation is then computed for each asset group. Using this approach, the auditor can easily approximate the correct amounts for the allowance and expense accounts.

A second objective is to examine the utilization of assets in order to evaluate the potential need for writing down the value of underutilized assets. If certain assets will be idled indefinitely, then they should be written off. The ratio of net property plant and equipment to sales can provide a useful measure of asset utilization for this purpose.

Accounts Payable, Unrecorded Liabilities, and Other Liabilities

The principal audit objective for these balance sheet accounts is to evaluate the completeness of the client's disclosure. Detail test procedures, including the analysis of payments after year-end, are the most useful for this purpose. However, analytical review can be used to supplement the detail procedures by indicating the extent of the pressures on management to understate liabilities to creditors and others. A good measure of the magnitude of these pressures is the current cash needs of the company. Three ratios, which are explained in Chapter 4, are well-suited for identifying severe cash needs:

$$\text{Acid-test ratio} = \frac{\text{cash} + \text{marketable securities} + \text{receivables}}{\text{current liabilities}}$$

$$\text{Defensive interval} = \frac{\text{cash} + \text{short-term marketable securities} + \text{receivables}}{\text{estimated daily cash operating expenditures (excludes depreciation)}}$$

$$\text{Payables turnover} = \frac{\text{accounts payable}}{\text{total disbursements}}$$

A significant unfavorable trend in any of these ratios could be an indication of critical cash need.

A second objective in this area is to evaluate the reasonableness of contingent liabilities. When the contingency is due to pending legal matters, the amount of the contingent liability is either well known or best assessed by legal opinion. So the auditor seeks legal advice on these matters. For other types of contingencies, such as one due to product warranties, the assessment of a reasonable contingency may be based on legal knowledge combined with a detailed analytical review. For example, product warranty costs may be a well-known proportion of total sales, adjusted for geographic location of sales and other factors. In this case, a careful reasonableness test should be appropriate, or a recompu-

Table 6-3 Inventory—Hypothetical Analytical Review Worksheet

Analytical Review Procedure	Product A				Product B			
	1980	1981	1982	1983	1980	1981	1982	1983
Part 1: Pricing, Obsolescence, Shrinkage								
Turnover ratio	9.2	9.6	9.5	10.1	8.6	8.1	8.0	7.5
Gross profit percentage	24.2	24.9	26.1	25.8	19.1	18.1	18.8	19.2
Raw materials turnover	5.9	6.5	4.8	6.0	8.8	6.0	6.5	6.2
Shrinkage rate, ratio of write-downs to total inventory	0.021	0.035	0.028	0.022	0.061	0.045	0.021	0.035
Analysis of standard cost budget variances; review of standard costs for reasonableness	N/A OK Not OK W/P ___	N/A OK Not OK W/P ___	N/A OK Not OK W/P ___	N/A OK Not OK W/P ___	N/A OK Not OK W/P ___	N/A OK Not OK W/P ___	N/A OK Not OK W/P ___	N/A OK Not OK W/P ___
Reasonableness test using average prices and units on hand to estimate current inventory value	OK Not OK W/P ___	OK Not OK W/P ___	OK Not OK W/P ___	OK Not OK W/P ___	OK Not OK W/P ___	OK Not OK W/P ___	OK Not OK W/P ___	OK Not OK W/P ___
Part 2: Misclassification, Cutoff								
Comparison of the ending balance in products for sale to budgeted sales	OK Not OK W/P ___	OK Not OK W/P ___	OK Not OK W/P ___	OK Not OK W/P ___	OK Not OK W/P ___	OK Not OK W/P ___	OK Not OK W/P ___	OK Not OK W/P ___
Comparison of the ending balance of raw materials to budgeted usage	OK Not OK W/P ___	OK Not OK W/P ___	OK Not OK W/P ___	OK Not OK W/P ___	OK Not OK W/P ___	OK Not OK W/P ___	OK Not OK W/P ___	OK Not OK W/P ___
Components of cost, %								
Materials	24.2	23.8	25.1	24.8	16.2	18.3	19.2	18.8
Labor	48.6	46.9	49.2	47.1	55.1	50.6	51.5	50.8
Overhead	27.2	29.3	25.7	28.1	28.7	31.1	29.3	30.4

Part 3: Other

Inspection for unusually large purchases near year-end	OK Not OK W/P ___	OK Not OK W/P ___	OK Not OK W/P ___	OK Not OK W/P ___	OK Not OK W/P ___	OK Not OK W/P ___	OK Not OK W/P ___
Roll-forward of beginning balance *plus* purchases *less* cost of sales (should approximately equal the ending balance)	OK Not OK W/P ___	OK Not OK W/P ___	OK Not OK W/P ___	OK Not OK W/P ___	OK Not OK W/P ___	OK Not OK W/P ___	OK Not OK W/P ___
A material adjustment in the account this year?	Yes No W/P ___	Yes No W/P ___	Yes No W/P ___	Yes No W/P ___	Yes No W/P ___	Yes No W/P ___	Yes No W/P ___
Other significant factors, such as turnover of key personnel?	Yes No W/P ___	Yes No W/P ___	Yes No W/P ___	Yes No W/P ___	Yes No W/P ___	Yes No W/P ___	Yes No W/P ___

tation of the client's figures, as is done in some cases for the allowance for doubtful accounts.

Revenue

Analytical review procedures can serve to address two of the audit objectives involved in the examination of revenue. The first is the test of the validity of the reported sales. Does the given amount represent legitimate sales for the accounting period? A second objective is to test for unrecorded sales. Unrecorded sales may occur if management wishes to lower tax liability, to smooth sales figures over different accounting periods, or the like.

The examination of the validity of sales is tested in part by procedures applied to other accounts, particularly accounts receivable and inventory. Thus, an unusual relationship detected in the examination of inventory or receivables may reflect an accounting problem for the reported sales figure as well. For example, unrecorded sales could be reflected in unusually high inventory shrinkage figures or an unusually low receivables turnover ratio. Because of these interrelationships, the auditor may wish to review sales at or about the same time that receivables and inventory are reviewed. Three procedures are appropriate for an examination of the validity of sales:

1. Examination of gross profit percentage. This ratio is compared with that of recent years for each major product line or segment. Unexplained large differences could be an indication of unreported or nonexistent sales.

2. Comparison of reported sales to budget. If available, a sales budget provides a valuable benchmark for evaluating actual sales performance. For the comparison to be most useful, the auditor must examine the reasonableness of the budget through knowledge of the company and its current market environment.

3. Reasonableness test of sales. The reasonableness test for sales resembles the roll-forward of finished goods inventory noted earlier for examining the reasonableness of the ending inventory balance. The auditor simply takes the units in beginning inventory of goods for sales, plus units completed in the current period, less ending inventory in units, to approximate the number of units sold this period. The production and sales units figures may be obtained from operations data and shipping documents, if not available with the financial records.

The examination for unrecorded sales would use the same three procedures. However, unrecorded sales are difficult to detect by analytical review since none of the financial records may be affected. For this reason the first two procedures above will probably not be as useful as the third, the reasonableness test, as it requires use of operating data which are more likely to show in some way the effect of unrecorded sales.

Two additional procedures may be useful in the analytical review of revenue:

1. Computation of the ratio of sales returns and allowances to sales. An unexpected change in this ratio from the prior period may indicate an accounting error in the treatment of this account.
2. Reasonableness test of investment income. The income from investments can most often be predicted quite easily and accurately from information about the invested amount and rate of return.

Expenses
The principal objective for the analytical review of the expense accounts is to evaluate whether each account is completely and properly stated. A preliminary approach to accomplish this would be to perform a trend analysis to isolate those accounts with unusual changes. The trend analysis is easy to apply and will be effective when all expense accounts are similarly affected by the factor or factors causing all the accounts to change. A significant problem in this regard is that expense accounts differ from one another in the proportion of "fixed" and "variable" cost components for the expense. For example, rent expense may be entirely fixed, whereas selling expense, when based primarily on commissions, would be largely variable in nature. This is a problem when applying trend analysis because a change in operating level will have a proportional change on variable expenses but no change on fixed expenses. The implication of this for the auditor is that the balance changes derived from trend analysis must be interpreted with an understanding of the nature of the expense under examination. Is it largely variable or fixed? And, should it have changed or not?

One way to avoid the above difficulty is to use a ratio analysis or reasonableness test approach for the review of the expense accounts. A suggested list of three types of ratio analysis and a variety of reasonableness test examples is given below:

1. *Ratio of expense account to related asset account.*
   a. Interest expense to debt.
   b. Depreciation expense to gross assets subject to depreciation.
   c. Bad debt expense to the allowance for bad debts.

    d. Repair and maintenance expense to related property, plant, and equipment accounts.

    e. Insurance expense to inventory plus property, plant, and equipment.

2. *Ratio of expense account to related expense account.*

    a. Payroll taxes to payroll expense.

    b. Employee benefit expense to payroll expense.

3. *Common-size income statement.*

    a. The ratio of each expense account to total sales. This type of ratio analysis, common-size income statements, is virtually equivalent to trend analysis, and it suffers from the same difficulty with respect to differences in the mix of variable and fixed costs across expense accounts. Thus, its use is subject to the interpretation problem noted above. The other two forms of ratio analysis are not subject to this problem and thus can be interpreted directly and easily.

4. *Reasonableness test.* Many expense accounts are easily estimated from one or a few items of relevant operating data. Illustrations of this method for fuel expense and for payroll expense were given in Chapter 5. Additional applications are:

    a. Depreciation expense, estimated from data for asset lives and depreciation methods, for homogeneous asset subgroups.

    b. Maintenance expense, estimated from floor space, direct labor hours, machine hours, and related operating data.

    c. Interest expense, estimated from relevant rates and debt amounts.

    d. Utilities expense, estimated from capacity utilization data, labor hours, possibly seasonally adjusted.

    e. Supplies expense, estimated from labor hours, machine hours, and related operating data.

Prepaid Expenses and Accrued Liabilities

Both these types of accounts represent the effect of year-end adjustments to achieve statements on the accrual basis of accounting. Thus, the audit objective is to see that the adjustments are complete and proper. Generally, the best approach for evaluating the accounts would be to employ a reasonableness test based upon relevant financial and operating data. This would involve approximating the amount of the related expense per week or month and then projecting this to the period necessary for the accrual. In some cases, the client's computation to arrive at the accrual may be simple enough that a full recomputation by the auditor may be the cost-effective approach. On the other hand, when the account balance comprises many items, as in the case of several different insurance policies—all prepaid with different premiums and periods of coverage—then a reasonableness test might be more appropriate. The auditor could estimate the premium per week for all policies and use approximated average accrual periods to compute an accrual estimate.

Similar methods would apply for the analyses of accrued liabilities. Recomputation or a reasonableness test is recommended, depending on the complexity of the account balance.

THE MULTIPLE LOCATION PROBLEM

Up to this point in the chapter we have been concerned with analytical review for account balances—to direct attention to those with a high potential for material misstatement or to provide evidence as a basis for reducing the scope of detail tests when the potential for misstatement appears to be low. Now, we turn our attention to a special case of the attention-directing role of analytical review which is used to *allocate* a given scope of audit effort rather than to *reduce or increase* scope, as we have done up to now.[1] This use of analytical review applies in those situations wherein the object of audit concern (say, inventory) is dispersed over two or more locations. Thus, it is called the "multiple location problem." A common example is the retailing company with many retail outlets. The audit question is, Which of the outlets should be examined? since it is not feasible or necessary to examine them all. We discuss here four approaches to resolving the question. The four are presented in increasing order of complexity, required expertise, and precision. The more precise methods will tend to be cost-beneficial on only the largest engagements owing to their complexity. The simpler methods should be useful in a wider range of applications. All methods involve in some way the evaluation and weighting of risk and materiality across all outlets. In describing each method, we will assume that we are analyzing the case of multiple retail outlets and that our objective is to allocate audit effort to inventory across outlets. Some outlets will be audited and others not.

The Direct Assessment Method

The first, and simplest, of the methods is that whereby the auditor makes a direct assessment of the risk associated with each outlet, and in this way derives a ranking of risk for the outlets. This ranking is used together with a measure of materiality of each outlet (this can be simply the dollar value of inventory at each outlet) to derive a ranking of a risk-weighted materiality measure for all outlets. This is illustrated in the hypothetical case shown in column 3 of Table 6-4.

The risk-weighted materiality measure can be used directly to determine which outlets to examine. For example, if audit scope calls for examining two outlets, then outlets A and B would be chosen since they have the highest values. If a third outlet is to be included, then outlet C would be chosen. Notice that the choice of outlets is different when using risk alone (column 1), materiality alone (column 2), or the risk-weighted materiality (column 3). Using column 3 is preferred since it incorporates both risk and materiality.

The Indirect Assessment Method

The indirect assessment method differs from the above in that the auditor directly assesses various *components* of risk and then aggregates these components to produce an indirect, overall risk assessment. This method is described in detail in Patton et al. (1982). The approach of Patton and his coworkers employs what is called the "analytical hierarchy method" to derive and combine the various attributes of overall risk. The method is somewhat complex. A simplified version of it is illustrated in Table 6-5. For simplicity, assume that the overall risk associated with an outlet comprises two major components—the quality of controls to safeguard inventory (control of inventory shrinkage) and the quality of internal control systems for cash receipts (prevention of unrecorded or misrecorded sales). The auditor makes a direct assessment of each component of risk in the same manner as used in the direct method. Then, a subjective relative weight is assigned to each of the two risk components to indicate the relative contribution of each to overall risk.

Table 6-4   The Multiple Location Problem—Direct Assessment Method

Outlet	Risk Assessed by Auditor* (1)	Materiality, Inventory Value, $ (2)	Risk-Weighted Materiality, $† (3)
A	2	550,000	1,100,000
B	4	160,000	640,000
C	3	150,000	450,000
D	1	435,000	435,000

*The risk measure is assessed by the auditor on a scale of 1 (lowest risk) to 7 (highest risk). The assessment is based upon the auditor's judgment, supported by knowledge of the personnel and quality of control systems in place at each outlet.
†(3) = (1) × (2).

Table 6-5 The Multiple Location Problem—Indirect Assessment Method

Out-let	Auditor's Assessment, Each Component of Risk*		Overall Risk Assessment (1)	Materiality, Inventory Value, $ (2)	Risk-Weighted Materiality, $§ (3)
	Safeguard Controls†	Cash Receipts Controls‡			
A	2	3	(2 × 2) + (3 × 1) = 7	550,000	3,850,000
B	5	2	(5 × 2) + (2 × 1) = 12	160,000	1,920,000
C	1	6	(1 × 2) + (6 × 1) = 8	150,000	1,200,000
D	1	2	(1 × 2) + (2 × 1) = 4	435,000	1,740,000

*The risk measure is assessed by the auditor on a scale of 1 (lowest risk) to 7 (highest risk).
†Relative weight = 2.0.
‡Relative weight = 1.0.
§(3) = (1) × (2).

If, for example, safeguard controls are twice as important as cash receipt controls, then the relative weights could be 2.0 and 1.0, respectively. Note that the amount of the weights is not important in itself; what is important is the relative values between weights, so that risk weights of 4.0 and 2.0 (for safeguard and cash controls, respectively) would produce results identical to the case where the risk weights are 2.0 and 1.0. That is, the ranking of overall risk would not be different.

The results of the indirect assessment method are shown in column 3 of Table 6-5. The overall risk-weighted materiality rankings indicate that outlet A should be investigated first and that B and D are of second priority. Alternatively, more time needs to be spent on outlet A, and correspondingly less time on B and D. Outlet C should get the least attention.

Statistical Risk Assessment

The statistical approach is comparable to what was described in Chapter 3 as the use of regression analysis to identify accounts with unexpected fluctuations. In the multiple location problem, the regression model is used to identify outlets with unexpected fluctuations or relationships.[2] The regression model is fitted from cross-sectional data from one point in time for all outlets. This means that there should be at least 10 to 12, and, ideally, 30 or more, outlets used to fit the regression to achieve an acceptably low level of sampling error. The dependent variable in the regression might be cost of sales, with the geographic area of the outlet, the size (floor space) of the outlet, and certain other attributes of the outlet (age, configuration, etc.) as independent variables. Another possible dependent variable is net sales, with similar independent variables. John Neter (1980) reports a case study in which a cross-sectional regression of this type was employed for the multiple location problem. His results are very interesting. The regression models have good predictive power even though data for some key independent variables were unavailable.[3] The evidence appears to be that the regression approach is very useful to the auditor in applications such as these.

Sequential Probability Ratio Method

Godfrey and Andrews (1980) have adapted the sequential probability ratio method for the multiple location audit problem. The method employs the precision of mathematical statistics to obtain a minimum cost allocation of sampling effort. The method is somewhat complex, but can be facilitated by interactive computer programming, as the authors indicate.

FOOTNOTES

[1]The term "allocate audit effort" can be considered quite broadly. It can refer to defining (1) which subset of a set of outlets will be examined, or (2) how much time to spend on each outlet, if all outlets are examined, or (3) which outlet to examine first, second, third, and so on. Typically, the audit decision is of the nature of (1) above, but the methods described for multiple location problems are applicable to each of the three forms of allocation.

[2]In the regression approach, an unusual outlet is identified by a large residual term for that outlet. The residual is the difference between the predicted value for the outlet and the actual value. This is explained more fully in Appendix 4.

[3]The predictive ability of the models, as measured by the coefficient of determination, was greater than 90 percent for five of the seven models; the other two had coefficients of 76 percent and 80 percent.

REFERENCES

Godfrey, James T., and Richard W. Andrews: "Testing Compliance at Multiple Sites: A Sequential Probability Ratio Model," Graduate School of Business Administration, University of Michigan, Ann Arbor, May 1980.

Kaplan, R. S.: "Developing a Financial Planning Model for an Analytic Review: A Replication," GSIA Working Paper 74-78-79, Carnegie-Mellon University, Pittsburgh, June 1979a.

_____: "Developing a Financial Planning Model for an Analytic Review: A Feasibility Study," in Symposium on Auditing Research III, University of Illinois, Urbana, 1979b.

_____: "A Financial Planning Model for an Analytical Review: The Case of a Savings and Loan Association," GSIA Working Paper 84-79-80, Carnegie-Mellon University, Pittsburgh, July 1980.

Neter, John: "Two Case Studies for Use of Regression for Analytic Review," in Symposium on Auditing Research IV, University of Illinois, Urbana, 1980.

Patton, James M., John H. Evans, III, and Barry L. Lewis: *A Framework for Evaluating Internal Audit Risk*, Institute of Internal Auditors Research Report 25, 1982.

chapter
seven

The Final
Analytical
Review

"The three princes of Serendip . . . were always making discoveries, by accidents and sagacity, of things they were not in quest of."

> Horace Walpole
> "The Three Princes of Serendip,"
> January 1754
> (in coining the term "serendipity")

The quality of serendipity is a good notion to begin this chapter on the final review phase for the audit engagement. Essentially, the reviewing audit partner applies "sagacity" to the review of the completed financial statements, to obtain additional assurance as to the reasonableness of the financial statements. The auditor at times and in a serendipitous fashion discovers unusual or unexpected relationships in the audited data which lead to further audit work to uncover accounting errors in the statements. Walpole's use of the term "sagacity" seems to fit here; it can be defined as a "discriminative intelligence," or an "acute, practical judgment," which leads to the serendipitous discovery.

Apart from the above, it is difficult to define that relatively specialized skill which the reviewing auditor applies in this final phase to detect problems not identified earlier in the planning and field work phases of the audit. The skill, it is argued, comes from in-depth knowledge of the client's business and accounting policies and procedures, which is derived in turn from extensive knowledge and experience in auditing.

Also, some argue that certain auditors are inherently better able to detect problems in this manner than are other auditors. The critical factors and relationships which identify the potential for material misstatement are more "transparent" for these auditors. However, no research we are aware of has been undertaken to determine if these experts exist, or what proportion of practicing auditors might be qualified as analytical review experts in some way. Additionally, none of the existing research has results which would be consistent with the hypothesis that some significant subpopulation of all auditors has these expert skills. The matter needs investigation, but at this point it seems unlikely we will find that a significant portion of auditors have substantially better analytical skills than others. Some suggestions for how firms or individual auditors can improve their skills are given in Chapter 8.

Now, we consider an approach and a set of procedures that the auditor can employ in the final review phase. Since the approach consists of a sequence of somewhat interdependent elements, we present it in the form of five steps.

STEP ONE

The auditor reviews the trend analysis on the working trial balance accounts, after correction for any adjustments and reclassifications. This will require recomputation of the amount and percentage trend used in planning, for the corrected amounts. Also, the auditor reviews the analytical review worksheets for inventory and accounts receivable, as illustrated in Chapter 6. Again, the figures in these worksheets are corrected for adjustments and reclassifications.

The auditor gives special attention to inventory and receivables since they are generally the most critical audit areas. If any other audit area is critical for the engagement (say, transactions with related parties for some companies), then there should be a review of the planning phase analytical review procedures in that area as well. Thus, the focus of the review is on the critical audit areas, with a brief review of the trend analysis for all accounts also being conducted.

The benefit of this overall review at the final stage is that sometimes a quick overview of all audit areas will uncover a potential problem when a detailed analysis in each area, taken one at a time, will not reveal the problem. Thus, something which might have been missed by a careful application of analytical review and detail tests in a given area might be identified when the results of the analytical review for all accounts are considered together, at one time. To accomplish this, the final review must be employed carefully, with sufficient quiet, reflective time for a thorough evaluation.

STEP TWO

The reviewing auditor should summarize all unexpected audit findings and try to tie them together. A review of the adjustment summary and memos of work done is useful at this point. Is there a pattern which leads to a significant audit concern not previously identified and addressed in the field work? For example, taken as a whole the audit findings may reflect a comprehensive strategy to lower the "quality" of earnings or the reported financial position through accounting and operating policies which tend to overstate assets and revenues and understate expenses and liabilities. To illustrate, the client may be putting off necessary maintenance and repairs, taking a very optimistic position on the collection rate for receivables, and experiencing an increase in the payables to disbursements ratio. Individually, the items would not be a concern, but in the aggregate they may be.

An important overall concern in this second step is for the reviewing auditor to be conscious of the *qualitative* rather than the quantitative value of the evidence. Because of checklists and other formal procedures, the quantity of evidence is likely to be complete, but it may be lacking in quality because of the inexperience of the staff assigned to the engagement. For example, the reviewing auditor should address the credibility of the data. To what extent does it rely on unsupported assertions of management, or upon data which have not been independently verified? This is particularly important when evaluating the results of analytical review procedures which may rely in part on unsupported assertions or data. We are aware of at least one case wherein an auditor was misled on the results of an analytical review because of reliance on incorrect operating data which later became the focus of litigation against the auditor.

STEP THREE

The auditor should reevaluate the going-concern status of the client, if appropriate, using the methods described in Chapter 2. The elements of operating risk and financial risk are particularly relevant at this time. The reviewing auditor can analyze certain financial ratios as indicators of financial distress and apply some of the financial distress models described in Chapter 2. See especially Tables 2-1 and 2-3.

Also, operating risk can be reevaluated by reference to the relevant indicators set forth in Chapter 2. In this regard, the auditor should try to anticipate potential significant events in the coming year which might have a substantial effect on financial position. Are all contingencies addressed and disclosed in the present draft of the statements and auditor's report? What regional economic trends, if any, are likely to affect the company in the coming year? Also, to what extent has management developed plans and procedures for dealing with contingencies? The existence of well-developed contingency plans is an offset to the degree of financial risk associated with the contingency.

STEP FOUR

The auditor should in addition reassess the management integrity issue, as described in Chapter 2. Has anything developed during the audit which should cause the auditor to question management's intentions? Is there evidence that management has tried to mislead the auditor on any matter? Further, are there reasons which would likely create a motivation for management to misrepresent the financial statements? Incentive-based executive compensation schemes, competition for promotion, personal financial distress, and related factors may have an impact on the motivations underlying management integrity on accounting matters.

STEP FIVE

The final step we suggest is to seek assistance of others with expertise in the client's industry and accounting systems. The objective of seeking assistance is primarily to improve the assessment of inherent risk and the related going-concern question, as noted above. The most convenient source for this would be others within the auditor's own firm who have the necessary expertise. Other sources include professional industry analysts, other financial analysts, local banking professionals, and industry publications. Useful references for this purpose include those noted in Chapter 2, plus *Standard and Poor's Industry Surveys,* and the Dow Jones–Irwin *Financial Analyst's Handbook II: Analysis by Industry* (edited by Sumner N. Levine). Each of the last two references includes 10 to 40 pages of detailed fundamental analysis of selected industry categories such as aerospace, chemicals, and so on. The Standard and Poor's *Survey* updates each industry analysis on a 1- to 2-year cycle.

chapter
eight

Analytical
Review
Guidance

This final chapter is the capstone for our efforts in the book. It sets forth our ideas and suggestions for enhancing the planning and usage of analytical review. The chapter serves as a guide for the auditor to develop a strategy for planning and using analytical review more effectively.

The strategy is a framework of concepts and knowledge which the auditor can apply to a given audit situation to answer certain basic questions about analytical review: *when* to employ it, *how* to employ it, and so on. In this manner, usage of analytical review should be enhanced:

1. The audit objective of analytical review will be more clear; the

results of analytical review will be better integrated into other audit work.

2. Documentation of analytical review will be improved.

3. There will be less tendency to use analytical review for no apparent purpose.

4. There will be increased usage of analytical review to reduce the scope of tests of details; by clarifying when and to what extent this role of analytical review applies, the framework will facilitate usage for this purpose.

5. There will be increased consensus among auditors in planning and usage of analytical review.

The chapter is organized as follows. There are two major objectives for the chapter. The first is to address the question "When does the auditor use and rely upon analytical review?" A guidance worksheet is developed for facilitating the auditor's consideration of this question, using the decision flowchart format. The guidance worksheet analyzes the question by identifying the five elements of the question and then formalizing the relationships between these elements.

The second objective of the chapter is to address the question "How does the auditor use analytical review most effectively?" Once the auditor has chosen to use analytical review, the question remains as to which analytical review procedure to apply and how to evaluate the results properly. This set of questions is addressed in two ways. First, there is a discussion of each of four analytical methods an auditor might employ. The discussion looks at the nature of each method to determine the required data and auditor expertise and uses this basis for determining what sorts of aids and guidance to give the auditor for the performance of each method. Second, there is a brief summary of the specific suggestions made in Chapters 2 through 5 regarding the proper use of trend analysis, ratio analysis, and reasonableness tests.

WHEN DOES THE AUDITOR USE AND RELY UPON ANALYTICAL REVIEW?

There are five elements to the question of when to use and rely upon analytical review. We discuss each element and incorporate it in a guidance worksheet. The five elements are (1) timing of analytical review, (2) the audit exposure associated with the account, (3) the objective of analytical review, either attention-directing or detail test–reducing, (4) the results of the analytical review, either an unexpected or an expected result; and (5) the precision of the review procedure. Each element is described briefly below.

Timing

Analytical review is usefully employed at the planning, field work, and final review phases of the audit engagement. It can also be used as a compensating test when the system of internal controls does not justify full reliance because of inadequate controls or compliance. The "compensating" analytical review can be used to justify a higher level of reliance when no unusual relationships or other signs of potential material error are identified by the review.

Exposure

Exposure is the audit significance of the account as measured by the combination of (1) the materiality of the account balance and (2) the audit risk for material misstatement in the account. The latter is determined from an evaluation of inherent risk and of the internal control risk for the account. What are the odds that a material error will occur in the account and not be detected by management's system of internal controls? These odds are the audit risk for the account. Exposure is greatest when the account is material in amount and audit risk is high. It is least when both materiality and risk are low.

Objective of Analytical Review

The objective of an analytical review is either to direct the auditor's attention to an account, item, or element of the financial statements where there is significant potential for misstatement, or to serve as a basis for reducing the scope of other tests. The priority placed on either of these two objectives depends in part on the evaluation of exposure. When exposure is high, the attention-directing objective is primary. But, when exposure is moderate or low, the test-reducing objective becomes primary. The primary and secondary objectives are illustrated by solid and dotted lines, respectively, in Figure 8-1, p. 148.

Analytical Review Results

Another important element of using analytical review effectively is the ability to interpret the results properly. When do the trend, ratio, or reasonableness test results indicate an unusual relationship, a sign of a potential material misstatement? In practice, the auditor determines a

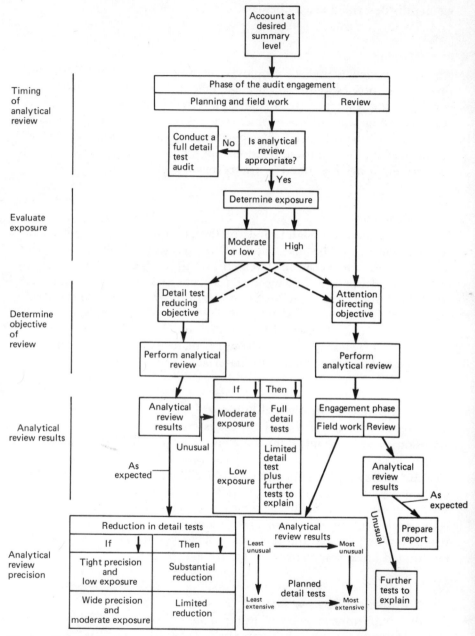

Figure 8-1 Guidance worksheet to determine when to use and rely upon analytical review.

threshold for the amount or percentage change or difference such that any change or difference greater than the threshold is considered unusual and further investigation is indicated. The choice of a threshold is a matter of judgment, and it is known to differ among industries and among clients of different sizes. A common rule is to use a threshold of 5 to 10 percent of net income, though rules based on assets or revenues are also in use.

Precision

Precision in the context of analytical review refers to the degree of confidence the auditor has in the prediction from the analytical review. Precision is influenced by the nature of the account, the nature of the analytical review procedure, and the accuracy of the data required by the analytical review procedure. In the first place, some accounts are simply more predictable than others. Depreciation expense is more predictable than maintenance expense, for example. Similarly, interest income is usually among the most easily predicted accounts.[1] A common aspect of the more predictable accounts is that at most one or two causal factors are involved in explaining the change in the balance over time. In the case of interest expense, for example, outstanding debt, period, and the relevant rate of interest are all that are necessary to explain interest expense fully. The more predictable an account is, the more precise is the analytical review.

A second component of precision is the nature of the procedure applied. Regression analysis is generally regarded as among the most precise of the procedures since it employs a best-fitting linear statistical method. Apart from this, it is difficult to generalize about the relative precision of the ratio, trend, and reasonableness test procedures. However, it can be argued that the reasonableness test is more precise than the others because it involves a formal modeling process based on operating data and other external data. In a similar vein, ratio analysis can be considered superior to a simple two-period trend analysis in that the ratio should capture some stable relationship between accounts, whereas many factors are involved in the one-period change in the balance. Also, an average of two or more predictions from different methods is often more accurate than a single prediction. By applying considerations such as these, the auditor must assess the relative precision of the procedure or procedures being employed.

The final component of precision is the degree of accuracy of the data used in the analytical review. This applies particularly to the reasonableness test or regression analysis, which require operating data and external data. If the data are of limited or unknown accuracy, the precision of the review is adversely affected.

The Guidance Worksheet

The guidance worksheet, Figure 8-1, ties all five elements together to develop a framework for choosing when to use and rely on analytical review. The worksheet is most easily used from top to bottom, beginning with the account under examination. At an early point in the decision flow the auditor must decide, "Is analytical review appropriate?" The point of this question is to eliminate such accounts as cash and the capital accounts which are most conveniently and effectively tested by detail methods. The worksheet continues from this point to show how the auditor can choose the appropriate level of detail testing under various combinations of the five key elements.

HOW TO USE ANALYTICAL REVIEW—
DEVELOPING AN APPROACH

It is more difficult to address the question of which analytical review procedure to choose and how to apply it than it is to identify the key elements in determining when to use analytical review, as we have done above. The "how" question is more difficult because a variety of procedures can be equally appropriate for a given situation. As a result, the auditor often completes two, three, or more analytical review procedures at the same time, as illustrated in the accounts receivable and inventory worksheets in Chapter 6.

For this reason, we have chosen to analyze the "how" question by studying the nature of four types of methods which can be used for analytical review. Three of the four are trend analysis, ratio analysis, and the reasonableness test, as described in Chapters 3, 4, and 5. The fourth, inherent risk analysis, is a term to summarize the variety of methods described in Chapter 2. A key aspect of inherent risk analysis is that the methods involve the application of accounting and business knowledge, often in a nonquantitative manner, to analyze the potential for material misstatement. In contrast, ratio, trend, and reasonableness tests are based on quantitative procedures.

Table 8-1 follows directly from this set of distinctions. It shows the extent to which judgment in applying the various analytical review methods is, or can be, aided by computational analysis, and, in cases involving computational analysis, whether regression analysis is used. It also shows the nature of auditor judgment when using each method, on a scale from "most subjective" to "most objective."

When one is considering methods that involve computational analysis (columns 2 and 3), it is important to know how the threshold is

Table 8-1   The Nature and Extent of Judgment When Using
Analytical Review

Analytical Review Method	Unaided by Computational Analysis (1)	Aided by Computational Analysis	
		Estimation of Thresholds Judgmentally (2)	Estimation of Thresholds by Regression Analysis (3)
1. Inherent risk analysis	X	X	
2. Ratio analysis		X	
3. Trend analysis		X	X
4. Reasonableness tests		X	X
Subjectivity versus objectivity level of the method		Most subjective (uses knowledge and experience only)	Most objective (uses structured mathematical methods)

source: Adapted from Blocher (1983); reprinted with permission of *CPA Journal,* copyright 1983, New York State Society of Certified Public Accountants.

determined. The threshold is the cutoff point used when applying the method that establishes whether a given amount or percent deviation is unusual or not.

Since most types of inherent risk analysis used in auditing are not computational, they do not involve a threshold. However, ratio analysis is computational, requiring judgment concerning the threshold for a significant deviation. Trend analysis and reasonableness tests are also computational and usually involve a threshold determined judgmentally. Moreover, these last two methods can be augmented by a regression analysis which provides a statistically determined threshold, the standard error of the estimate.

For purposes of developing a framework of guidance that will help the auditor answer the "how" question, we consider the three columns in Table 8-1 to represent three different "approaches" to analytical review which differ on a subjective-objective dimension as indicated.

The differences between approaches can be directly related to differences in the nature of the required guidance and support to be given to the auditor.[2] For example, since approach 1 encompasses a broad range of methods which require a substantial amount of accounting and business knowledge, it follows that major concerns are:

1. The *consensus* among auditors concerning how this approach is applied

2. The *consistency* with which any given auditor applies the approach over time

3. The *completeness* and thoroughness with which the approach is applied

The choice of an appropriate form of guidance for auditors when using approach 1 should address these three concerns. For example, one could attend to the objectives of consensus and consistency by requiring the auditor to use a list of suggested analyses that are commonly used in effective risk analysis. The listing would primarily serve as a reminder of possible analyses rather than as a device to restrict the auditor's judgment in a predetermined manner since the auditor in the field is best able to choose the form of analysis for a particular engagement. Also, the guidance objective of completeness could be addressed by making training materials and relevant databases readily available in a very easy-to-use form. This discussion is summarized in Table 8-2.

In approach 2 the guidance objectives of consensus and consistency still apply, but the objective of completeness is less relevant since the methods applied are more well defined. Thus, experience and training are relatively less important. However, approach 2 often involves lengthy, tedious calculations, such as those necessary for a trend analysis of the working trial balance accounts. Thus, a relevant objective here is to reduce the amount of arithmetic required of the auditor. In consideration of these objectives, support for approach 2 might include the following:

1. Computer-assisted preparation of "exception schedules" which highlight significant deviations from expected trends and ratios.

2. Computer-assisted sensitivity analyses and "what if" analyses. For example, a "what if" analysis could be used to show the effect on the client's current ratio if a certain contingent liability is realized shortly after the report date.

3. Computer-based client and industry data, to facilitate various analyses.

4. Guidance for deciding when a fluctuation or deviation from the expected value is significant and what adjustments to audit scope are necessary in this event.

When one is considering guidance for approach 3, the issues of consensus and consistency are not important because they are provided by the structure involved in applying the regression model. However, there are two new objectives:

1. The regression analysis must be done properly, and the results must be interpreted properly.
2. The auditor must be satisfied that the data used to fit the regression model are both accurate and comparable across different time periods.

These objectives can be achieved by providing an interactive computer program to solve the regression model. The computer can also be used to present the results in a manner designed to facilitate proper interpretation. For example, a set of questions could be used. The auditor would have to answer the questions correctly to receive the final regression results. Alternatively, the regression results could include a diagnostic report, in simple language, which would advise the auditor of problems such as an ill-defined model and the implication of those problems for interpreting the results.

USING ANALYTICAL REVIEW—SUMMARY NOTES

The objective of this final portion of the chapter is to summarize relevant aspects of Chapters 2 through 5 which bear upon the effective use of trend analysis, ratio analysis, and the reasonableness test. The reader should refer to these previous chapters for a more thorough treatment of these points.

Trend Analysis

Our survey of research into the judgments of auditors and others, in contexts related to the trend analysis task, has identified six concerns that the auditor should be alert to when performing a trend analysis task and interpreting its results. A useful broad survey of this research is given by Hogarth and Makridakis (1981) and by Libby (1981).

1. The confirmation bias. Decision makers in a wide variety of decision contexts have shown a bias favoring the apparent hypothesis. There is a tendency not to seek out disconfirming evidence, nor to search for alternate explanations for what appears to be an obvious interpretation of results. For example, an auditor might be inclined to accept the generic explanation of "inflation" to explain rising costs, when a closer examination of operating data might show that costs in fact should have declined.

Table 8-2 Requirements, Objectives, and Suggested Support Aids for Each Analytical Review Approach

		Aided by Computational Analysis	
	Unaided by Computational Analysis (1)	Estimation of Thresholds Judgmentally (2)	Estimation of Thresholds by Regression Analysis (3)
Requirements			
Knowledge	A substantial amount of knowledge about (1) the client's organization and business and (2) the financial and operating relationships of the client.	Same as for (1), plus knowledge of how to apply the chosen method properly.	An understanding of regression analysis: 1. How to apply it properly. 2. How to interpret the results.
Data	1. Client financial and operating data. 2. Other client data: correspondence, minutes of meetings, and so on.	Client financial and operating data.	1. Reliable time-series data for the account being analyzed. 2. Reliable operating and financial data for the account being analyzed.
Computation	Typically negligible.	Tedious; sometimes voluminous; arithmetically simple.	Done by a computer program.
Objectives			
	1. Consensus. 2. Consistency. 3. Completeness.	1. Consensus. 2. Consistency. 3. Removal of the burden of tedious computations.	1. Proper application of the model and interpretation of the model's results. 2. Use of accurate and comparable data.

Aids

1. A listing of risk analyses. The auditor should provide responses explaining (a) which measures the auditor feels are appropriate, (b) the work done, and (c) the auditor's conclusion. 2. Easy access to training materials and databases.	1. Computer-assisted preparation of exception schedules, given the auditor's desired threshold. 2. Computer-assisted sensitivity analyses and "what if" analyses. 3. Computer-stored databases of client and industry data. 4. Guidance for deciding when a fluctuation or deviation from the expected value is significant, and the nature of further audit work, if any.	1. An interactive computer program for solving the mathematics of regression. 2. In connection with the computer program, a set of questions to test the program user's proper understanding of the program and proper interpretation of the results. 3. Guidance for evaluating the accuracy and comparability of the operating data. 4. Accurate industry and economic data.

SOURCE: Adapted from Blocher (1983). Reprinted with permission of *CPA Journal*, copyright 1983, New York State Society of Certified Public Accountants.

Auditors should be conscious of this pervasive judgment bias. One way to respond to it is to use a *causal reasoning* approach in analytical review. By this approach, the auditor predicts what the balance or relationship should have been for the current year, using as a basis for the prediction operating and external data, and then compares the predicted and reported amounts for reasonableness. In contrast, auditors have often taken a *diagnostic* approach wherein the current balances are reviewed for reasonableness, with no explicit prediction involved. This latter approach causes the auditor to be more prone to the confirmation bias since it does not require an assessment of relevant operating and external data.

2. Studies have shown that auditors and others tend to overestimate the degree of trend to a series of numbers. Their "intuitive" predictions are biased too high.

3. Studies have shown that auditors and others tend to underestimate the degree of variability in a series of numbers. As a result, they are overconfident as to the accuracy of their predictions.

4. Simple quantitative prediction models tend to outperform unaided human decision makers, a fact which is consistent with items 2 and 3. This suggests that auditors should be cautioned about using a strictly intuitive approach to prediction; some of the simple quantitative trend analysis methods shown in Chapter 3 should be used as well.

5. The simple quantitative models discussed in item 4 have been found to be as accurate as or better than more complex models in a wide variety of contexts. This suggests that one or a few independent variables will be sufficient for many of the prediction models the auditor will need.

6. Our research results indicate that auditors tend to base their judgments about whether or not a given change in an account balance is significantly unusual upon the amount of the change rather than upon the percent change from the prior year. This means that auditors will potentially underweight the significance of deviations in small accounts.

Ratio Analysis

The discussion in Chapter 4 includes the three assumptions and limitations involved in using ratio analysis:

1. When comparing the ratio with either a prior year's ratio or an industry average, the auditor should ensure that the comparison is appropriate. There are two reasons why the ratios may not be comparable. First, two ratios being compared may have been computed differently. Second, there may be differences in the accounting policies and conventions used to prepare the account balances in the ratios. For example, inventory turnover ratios may differ because of differences in accounting methods for inventory—LIFO or FIFO, the cost accounting method (including the treatment of overhead), and the treatment of obsolete or damaged inventory.

2. For a ratio comparison to be meaningful, the relationship between the numerator *(y)* and the denominator *(x)* must be strictly *linear;* that is, a given change in the denominator must produce a predictable amount of change in the numerator. Also, the relationship between the numerator and denominator must be strictly variable; that is, the intercept term "a" in the linear model relating the two must be equal to zero. In symbols, $y = a + bx$ becomes $y = bx$, and the ratio $b = y/x$ reflects the assumed strictly linear, strictly variable relationship between x and y.

The strict variability assumption is often violated by ratios of certain expense accounts to total sales or total expenses. Whenever an expense has a fixed-cost component, the ratio does not reflect a strictly variable relationship.

The assumption of a strictly linear relationship is sometimes inappropriate as well. For example, when the economic order quantity (EOQ) formula is used to determine inventory levels, the inventory turnover ratio is nonlinear. The reason for this is that the EOQ formula prescribes a relationship between the level of inventory and the *square root* of sales, and thus the ratio is not linear.

3. A variety of operating and financing differences between firms can cause ratios to be noncomparable. Differences in such factors as production technologies, capacity utilization, geographic location, financial leverage, and growth rate would cause a firm's ratios to be noncomparable with those of other firms.

Reasonableness Tests

It is difficult to generalize about the potential problems in using the reasonableness test method since the exact form of the reasonableness test will differ substantially in different applications. However, two general observations should be useful to the auditor. First, our work with auditors indicates that many auditors always assume a linear, additive relationship between variables, though in some cases a nonlinear or multiplicative relationship is involved. For example, total payroll expenses can be predicted by multiplying wage rate, hours worked, and number of employees. Many auditors have mistakenly modeled these variables in an additive form.

Second, when one is using a reasonableness test, it is important to identify *all* the variables which are relevant for predicting the account balance. Failure to identify a complete model will result in relatively inaccurate predictions and overconfidence in the precision of the predictions.

Exhibit 4 illustrates a guidance form which can be used to facilitate proper application of the reasonableness test in analyzing payroll expense. Similar guidance forms could be developed for such accounts as maintenance expense, utilities and fuel expense, depreciation expense, and so on.

FOOTNOTES

[1]We are using the term "predictable" in the "ex post" sense; that is, we are interested in the ability to predict, after the close of the account period, what the account balance *should* be, as in the typical audit context. The ability to predict the account balance at some future time is a far different matter and is not directly relevant for the auditor's use of analytical review.

[2]Libby (1981) surveys the research which has been done to investigate the effectiveness of various forms of guidance. Relatively little research of this type has been done in an accounting or auditing context. Important papers on the topic in the psychological literature are those by Hogarth and Makridakis (1981) and Einhorn (1972).

REFERENCES

Blocher, Edward: "Approaching Analytical Review," *CPA Journal*, March 1983, pp. 24–32.

_____ and Andy Luzi: "Guidance Effects on Analytical Review Decisions," unpublished working paper, University of North Carolina, Chapel Hill, September 1983.

Einhorn, Hillel J.: "Expert Judgment and Mechanical Combination," *Organizational Behavior and Human Performance*, February 1972, pp. 86–106.

Hogarth, Robin M., and Spyros Makridakis: "The Value of Decision Making in a Complex Environment: An Experimental Approach," *Management Science*, January 1981, pp. 93–107.

Libby, Robert: *Accounting and Human Information Processing: Theory and Application*, Prentice-Hall, Englewood Cliffs, N.J., 1981.

EXHIBIT 4

ILLUSTRATIVE REASONABLENESS TEST GUIDANCE FOR PAYROLL EXPENSE

1. OBJECTIVES

a. To analyze the relationships between relevant financial, operating, and economic data to aid the auditor in making an independent prediction of the payroll account.

b. To use the predicted payroll expense balance in making an assessment as to the possibility of a material error in the unaudited payroll expense account.

2. PROBLEM IDENTIFICATION

a. Obtain the prior year's audited account balance and this year's unaudited account balance.

b. Calculate the difference between these account balances. Is this difference in line with the financial, operating, and economic factors related to this account?

3. MODEL DEVELOPMENT AND PREDICTION FOR PAYROLL EXPENSE. (The analysis that follows is designed to assess the potential that an error exists that could materially affect the financial statements. Note that the above comparison of current and prior year's balances, alone, is not sufficient because of financial, operating, and economic changes between years. Thus, the analysis requires the prediction of the current balance using relevant financial, operating, and economic information.)

a. MODEL

Factors to consider when analyzing the relationships affecting payroll expense:

- Wage rates
- Idle time
- Overtime
- Number of employees
- Other factors relevant to this account balance:

_____

_____

The *type* of predictive relationship (model) applicable to this case is:

Predicted expense = prior-year audited expense × a predicted percent adjustment for the effect of any changes in the above factors for the year.

Using the above general information and the specific facts of the audit, write out the predictive relationship you will use for this audit to predict payroll expense:

Payroll Expense = _____

_____

_____

_____

b. ACCEPTANCE CRITERIA

Select acceptance criteria that will indicate a possibility of material error in the payroll expense account when compared with the difference (or percent/relationship) between the current-year unaudited payroll expense and the predicted balance in the payroll expense account.

c. PREDICTION

(1) Obtain the required information:

- Prior-year audited
  payroll expense   _____
- Wage rates   _____
- Idle time   _____
- Overtime   _____
- Number of employees   _____
- Other information:

  _____

  _____

(2) Compute the predicted account balance using the model in **3.a.** and the data immediately preceding:

_____

_____

_____

_____

Predicted account balance $ _____

4. DECISION ANALYSIS

a. Calculate a "predicted difference" by subtracting the predicted account balance from the current unaudited account balance.

b. Compare the predicted difference with the difference criteria for acceptance in **3.b.**

c. On the basis of this comparison, determine the nature and extent of any further audit work needed.

SOURCE: Adapted from Blocher and Luzi (1983).

appendix one

SAS 23, "Analytical Review Procedures"

.01 This section applies to analytical review procedures in an examination made in accordance with generally accepted auditing standards.[1] It provides guidance for consideration by the auditor when he applies such procedures, but no specific analytical review procedures are required by this section.

.02 Analytical review procedures are substantive tests of financial information made by a study and comparison of relationships among data. The auditor's reliance on substantive tests may be derived from tests of details of transactions and balances, from analytical review procedures, or from any combination of both. That decision is a matter

---

[1]This section amends the first sentence of section 320.70 to read as follows: The evidential matter required by the third standard is obtained through two general classes of auditing procedures: (a) tests of details of transactions and balances and (b) analytical review procedures applied to financial information.

of the auditor's judgment of the expected effectiveness and efficiency of the respective types of procedures. . . .

.03 A basic premise underlying the application of analytical review procedures is that relationships among data may reasonably be expected by the auditor to exist and continue in the absence of known conditions to the contrary. The presence of those relationships provides the auditor with evidential matter required by the third standard of field work. The application of analytical review procedures may indicate the need for additional procedures or may indicate that the extent of other auditing procedures may be reduced.

.04 When analytical review procedures identify fluctuations that are not expected, or the absence of fluctuations when they are expected, or other items that appear to be unusual, the auditor should investigate them if he believes that they are indicative of matters that have a significant effect on his examination.

Timing and Objectives of Analytical Review Procedures

.05 The timing of analytical review procedures will vary with the auditor's objectives. Analytical review procedures may be performed at various times during an examination:

a. In the initial planning stages to assist in determining the nature, extent, and timing of other auditing procedures by identifying, among other things, significant matters that require consideration during the examination.
b. During the conduct of the examination in conjunction with other procedures applied by the auditor to individual elements of financial information.
c. At or near the conclusion of the examination as an overall review of the financial information.

The Nature of Analytical Review Procedures

.06 Analytical review procedures include the following:

a. Comparison of the financial information with information for comparable prior period(s).
b. Comparison of the financial information with anticipated results (for example, budgets and forecasts).
c. Study of the relationships of elements of financial information that

would be expected to conform to a predictable pattern based on the entity's experience.

d. Comparison of the financial information with similar information regarding the industry in which the entity operates.

e. Study of relationships of the financial information with relevant nonfinancial information.

Various methods may be used to perform these procedures. They may be made using dollars, physical quantities, ratios, or percentages. The methods selected by the auditor are a matter of his professional judgment.

.07 Analytical review procedures may be applied to overall financial information of the entity, to financial information of components such as subsidiaries or divisions, and to individual elements of financial information. The auditor should consider the following factors when planning and performing analytical review procedures.

a. *The nature of the entity.* For example, an auditor performing an examination of a diversified entity may conclude that the application of analytical review procedures to the consolidated financial statements may not be as effective or efficient as the application of those procedures to the consolidated financial statements of a nondiversified entity.

b. *The scope of the engagement.* For example, an examination of a specified element, account, or item of a financial statement may include fewer analytical review procedures than would an examination of financial statements.

c. *The availability of financial information about the entity's financial position and results of operations.* Examples may include budgets and forecasts and detailed financial information about the entity's subsidiaries or divisions and interim periods.

d. *The availability of relevant nonfinancial information.* Examples may include units produced or sold, number of employees, hours worked by nonsalaried personnel, and square feet of selling floor space, which may be related to financial information.

e. *The reliability of financial and nonfinancial information.* The auditor should consider the possibility that financial or nonfinancial information might not be reliable based on his knowledge of the entity, including his knowledge of the means by which the information is produced. In that connection, the auditor should consider knowledge obtained during previous examinations, the results of his study and evaluation of internal accounting control, and the results of his tests of details of transactions and balances. He should consider the types of matters that in preceding periods have required accounting adjustments. For example, the auditor may decide not to conduct certain analytical review procedures until near the completion of his examination if he is aware that trial balance amounts may require substantial adjustments; or he may decide to make only limited comparisons of actual and budgeted income and expense when the entity's budget is a motivational tool and not an estimate of the most probable financial position, results of operations, and changes in financial position.

f. *The availability and comparability of financial information regarding the industry in which the entity operates.* The auditor should consider whether industry information, such as gross margin information, is reasonably available and current and whether data used to compile the information is comparable to the information being evaluated. For example, broad industry information may not be comparable to that of an entity that produces and sells specialized products.

Investigating Significant Fluctuations

.08 The auditor should investigate fluctuations that are not expected, the absence of fluctuations that are expected, and other items that appear to be unusual that are identified by analytical review procedures when he believes that those fluctuations or unusual items are indicative of matters that have a significant effect on his examination. When investigating such significant fluctuations, the auditor ordinarily would begin by making suitable inquiries of management. He would then *(a)* evaluate the reasonableness of replies to his inquiries by reference to his knowledge of the business and other information already obtained during the conduct of the examination and *(b)* consider the need to corroborate the replies to his inquiries by the application of other auditing procedures. If management is unable to provide an acceptable explanation of significant fluctuations, the auditor should perform additional procedures to investigate those fluctuations further.

.09 In deciding the nature and extent of procedures which should be used to investigate significant fluctuations, the auditor's consideration should include the following factors:

a. *The objective of the analytical review procedures.* For example, the objective may be to assist the auditor in planning his examination by identifying areas that may need special consideration (such as identifying any significant increases in inventories by inventory locations). The extent to which the auditor decides to corroborate an explanation of a significant fluctuation in those circumstances depends on whether the resulting audit plan he develops would otherwise provide sufficient evidential matter.

b. *The nature of the item.* For example, an auditor investigating a fluctuation in inventory turnover in a manufacturing company might corroborate a response to his inquiry by obtaining other evidential matter, such as evidence with respect to unusual quantities of inventories represented to be on hand at the date of the financial statements. Conversely, an auditor might limit to inquiries his investigation of a fluctuation in prepaid insurance for the same company.

c. *The auditor's knowledge of the entity's business.* For example, the auditor may be aware of an extended strike by manufacturing employees during the year. He may conclude that this is a satisfactory explanation for a decline in sales volume and not apply other procedures to investigate this otherwise significant fluctuation.

d. *The results of other auditing procedures.* For example, the auditor may decide not to apply other procedures to investigate an otherwise significant fluctuation in depreciation expense because he may already be aware of major additions or retirements from his tests of property transactions.

e. *The auditor's study and evaluation of internal accounting control.* For example, the extent to which the auditor decides to corroborate an explanation of an increase in bad debt expense may vary depending on his evaluation of internal accounting control in the credit department.

.10 In his investigation of significant fluctuations, the auditor also should be alert to the possible effect of his findings on the scope of his examination of related accounts. For example, a finding that accounts receivable have increased due to slow collections in a "tight money" environment may indicate the need for expanded tests of collectibility.

appendix two

Selected Paragraphs from *SSARS 1*, "Compilation and Review of Financial Statements"

Review of Financial Statements

.24 The accountant should possess a level of knowledge of the accounting principles and practices of the industry in which the entity operates and an understanding of the entity's business that will provide him, through the performance of inquiry and analytical procedures, with a reasonable basis for expressing limited assurance that there are no material modifications that should be made to the financial statements in order for the statements to be in conformity with generally accepted accounting principles. (. . . , reference to generally accepted accounting principles in this statement includes, where applicable, another comprehensive basis of accounting.)

.25 The requirement that the accountant possess a level of knowledge of the accounting principles and practices of the industry in which the entity operates does not prevent an accountant from accepting a review engagement for an entity in an industry with which the accountant has no previous experience. It does, however, place upon the accountant a responsibility to obtain the required level of knowledge. He may do so, for example, by consulting AICPA guides, industry publications, financial statements of other entities in the industry, textbooks and periodicals, or individuals knowledgeable about the industry.

.26 The accountant's understanding of the entity's business should include a general understanding of the entity's organization, its operating characteristics, and the nature of its assets, liabilities, revenues, and expenses. This would ordinarily involve a general knowledge of the entity's production, distribution, and compensation methods, types of products and services, operating locations, and material transactions with related parties. An accountant's understanding of an entity's business is ordinarily obtained through experience with the entity or its industry and inquiry of the entity's personnel.

.27 The accountant's inquiry and analytical procedures should ordinarily consist of the following:

a. Inquiries concerning the entity's accounting principles and practices and the methods followed in applying them.

b. Inquiries concerning the entity's procedures for recording, classifying, and summarizing transactions, and accumulating information for disclosure in the financial statements.

c. Analytical procedures designed to identify relationships and individual items that appear to be unusual. For the purposes of this statement, analytical procedures consist of (1) comparison of the financial statements with statements for comparable prior period(s), (2) comparison of the financial statements with anticipated results, if available (for example, budgets and forecasts), and (3) study of the relationships of the elements of the financial statements that would be expected to conform to a predictable pattern based on the entity's experience. In applying these procedures, the accountant should consider the types of matters that required accounting adjustments in preceding periods. Examples of relationships of elements in financial statements that would be expected to conform to a predictable pattern may be the relationships between changes in sales and changes in accounts receivable and expense accounts that ordinarily fluctuate with sales, and between changes in property, plant, and equipment and changes in depreciation expense and other accounts that may be affected, such as maintenance and repairs.

d. Inquiries concerning actions taken at meetings of stockholders, board of directors, committees of the board of directors, or comparable meetings that may affect the financial statements.

e. Reading the financial statements to consider, on the basis of information coming to the accountant's attention, whether the financial statements appear to conform with generally accepted accounting principles.

f. Obtaining reports from other accountants, if any, who have been engaged to audit or review the financial statements of significant components of the reporting entity, its subsidiaries, and other investees.

g. Inquiries of persons having responsibility for financial and accounting matters concerning (1) whether the financial statements have been prepared in conformity with generally accepted accounting principles consistently applied, (2) changes in the entity's business activities or accounting principles and practices, (3) matters as to which questions have arisen in the course of applying the foregoing procedures, and (4) events subsequent to the date of the financial statements that would have a material effect on the financial statements.

.28 Knowledge acquired in the performance of audits of the entity's financial statements, compilation of the financial statements, or other accounting services may result in modification of the review procedures described in the preceding paragraph. However, such modification would not reduce the degree of responsibility the accountant assumes with respect to the financial statements he has reviewed.

.29 A review does not contemplate a study and evaluation of internal accounting control, tests of accounting records and of responses to inquiries by obtaining corroborating evidential matter, and certain other procedures ordinarily performed during an audit. Thus, a review does not provide assurance that the accountant will become aware of all significant matters that would be disclosed in an audit. However, if the accountant becomes aware that information coming to his attention is incorrect, incomplete or otherwise unsatisfactory, he should perform the additional procedures he deems necessary to achieve limited assurance that there are no material modifications that should be made to the financial statements in order for the statements to be in conformity with generally accepted principles.

.30 Although it is not possible to specify the form or content of the working papers that an accountant should prepare in connection with a review of financial statements because of the different circumstances of individual engagements, the accountant's working papers should describe:

a. The matters covered in the accountant's inquiry and analytical procedures.

b. Unusual matters that the accountant considered during the performance of the review, including their disposition.

appendix
three

Selected Paragraphs from *SAS 36*, "Review of Interim Financial Statements"

OBJECTIVE OF A REVIEW OF INTERIM FINANCIAL INFORMATION

.03 The objective of a review of interim financial information is to provide the accountant, based on objectively applying his knowledge of financial reporting practices to significant accounting matters of which he becomes aware through inquiries and analytical review procedures, with a basis for reporting whether material modifications should be made for such information to conform with generally accepted accounting principles. The objective of a review of interim financial information differs significantly from the objective of an examination of financial statements in accordance with generally accepted auditing standards. The objective of an audit is to provide a reasonable basis for expressing an opinion regarding the financial statements taken as a whole. A review of interim financial information does not provide a basis for the expression of such an opinion, because the review does not contemplate a study and evaluation of internal accounting control: tests of accounting records and of responses to inquiries by obtaining corroborating evidential matter through inspection, observation, or confirmation; and certain other procedures ordinarily performed during an audit. A review may bring to the accountant's attention significant matters affecting the interim financial information, but it does not provide assurance that the accountant will become aware of all significant matters that would be disclosed in an audit.

PROCEDURES FOR A REVIEW OF INTERIM FINANCIAL INFORMATION

.04 The characteristics of interim financial information necessarily affect the nature, timing, and extent of procedures that the accountant may apply in making a review of that information. Timeliness is an important element of interim financial reporting. Interim financial information customarily is made available to investors and others more promptly than is annual financial information. Timely reporting of interim financial information ordinarily precludes the development of information and documentation underlying interim financial information to the same extent as that underlying annual financial information. Therefore, a characteristic of interim financial information is that many costs and expenses are estimated to a greater extent than for annual financial reporting purposes. Another characteristic of interim financial information is its relationship to annual financial reporting purposes. Deferrals, accruals, and estimates at the end of each interim period are affected by judgments made at interim dates concerning anticipated results of operations for the remainder of the annual period.

.05 The procedures for a review of interim financial information are described in the following paragraphs concerning the (a) nature of procedures (paragraph **.06**), (b) timing of procedures (paragraph **.07**), and (c) extent of procedures (paragraphs **.08** through **.15**).

NATURE OF PROCEDURES

.06 Procedures for making a review of interim financial information consist primarily of inquiries and analytical review procedures concerning significant accounting matters relating to the financial information to be reported. The procedures that the accountant ordinarily should apply are:

a. Inquiry concerning (1) the accounting system, to obtain an understanding of the manner in which transactions are recorded, classified, and summarized in the preparation of interim financial information, and (2) any significant changes in the system of internal accounting control, to ascertain their potential effect on the preparation of interim financial information.

b. Application of analytical review procedures to interim financial information to identify and provide a basis for inquiry about relationships and individual items that appear to be unusual. Analytical review procedures, for purposes of this section, consist of (1) comparison of the financial information with comparable information for the immediately preceding interim period and for corresponding previous period(s), (2) comparison of the financial information with anticipated results, and (3) study of the relationships of elements of financial information that would be expected to conform to a predictable pattern based on the entity's experience. In applying these procedures, the accountant should consider the types of matters that in the preceding year or quarters have required accounting adjustments.

c. Reading the minutes of meetings of stockholders, board of directors, and committees of the board of directors to identify actions that may affect the interim financial information.

d. Reading the interim financial information to consider, on the basis of information coming to the accountant's attention, whether the information to be reported conforms with generally accepted accounting principles.

e. Obtaining reports from other accountants, if any, who have been engaged to make a review of the interim financial information of significant components of the reporting entity, its subsidiaries, or other investees.

f. Inquiry of officers and other executives having responsibility for financial and accounting matters concerning (1) whether the interim financial information has been prepared in conformity with generally accepted accounting principles consistently applied, (2) changes in the entity's business activities or accounting practices, (3) matters as to which questions have arisen in the course of applying the foregoing procedures, and (4) events subsequent to the date of the interim financial information that would have a material effect on the presentation of such information.

g. Obtaining written representations from management concerning its responsibility for the financial information, completeness of minutes, subsequent events, and other matters for which the accountant believes written representations are appropriate in the circumstances.

TIMING OF PROCEDURES

.07 Adequate planning by the accountant is essential to the timely completion of a review of interim financial information. Performance of some of the work before the end of the interim period may permit the work to be carried out in a more efficient manner and to be completed at an earlier date. Performing some of the work earlier in the interim period also permits early consideration of significant accounting matters affecting the interim financial information.

EXTENT OF PROCEDURES

.08 The extent to which the procedures referred to in paragraph **.06** are applied depends on the considerations described in paragraphs **.09** through **.15.**

The Accountant's Knowledge of Accounting and Reporting Practices

.09 Knowledge of a client's accounting and financial reporting practices is an important factor in the performance of a review of interim financial information. An understanding of a client's practices in preparing its most recent annual financial statements provides a practical basis for the inquiry and other procedures of a review. Such an understanding can be expected to have been acquired by the accountant who has audited a client's financial statements for one or more annual periods.

The Accountant's Knowledge of Weaknesses in Internal Accounting Control

.10 An accountant who has previously made an audit of his client's financial statements will have acquired knowledge concerning his client's system of internal accounting control relating to the preparation of financial statements, generally for an annual period. In these circumstances, the primary objective of the accountant's inquiries should be to identify and consider the effect of (a) changes in the system subsequent to his examination and (b) accounting control procedures used in the preparation of interim financial information that differ from those used in the preparation of annual financial statements. If the system of internal accounting control appears to contain weaknesses that do not permit preparation of interim financial information in conformity with generally accepted accounting principles, and, as a consequence, it is impracticable for the accountant to effectively apply his knowledge of financial reporting practices to the interim financial information, he should consider whether the weaknesses represent a restriction on the scope of his engagement sufficient to preclude completion of such a review. The accountant should also advise senior management and the board of directors or its audit committee of the circumstances; he may also wish to submit suggestions regarding other weaknesses in the system of internal accounting control, recommendations for improvement of interim reporting practices, and any other matters of significance that come to his attention.

The Accountant's Knowledge of Changes in Nature or Volume of Activity or Accounting Changes

.11   A review of interim financial information may bring to the accountant's attention changes in the nature or volume of the client's business activities or accounting changes. Examples of changes that could affect the interim financial information to be reported include business combinations: disposal of a segment of the business; extraordinary, unusual, or infrequently occurring transactions; initiation of litigation or the development of other contingencies; trends in sales or costs that could affect accounting estimates relating to the valuations of receivables and inventories, realization of deferred charges, provisions for warranties and employee benefits, and unearned income; and changes in accounting principles or in the methods of applying them. If any such changes come to the accountant's attention, he should inquire about the manner in which the changes and their effects are to be reported in the interim financial information.

Issuance of Accounting Pronouncements

.12   The accountant's knowledge of financial reporting practices is expected to include an awareness of new pronouncements on financial accounting standards. In performing a review of interim financial information he should consider the applicability of any such new pronouncements to his client's interim financial reporting practices. The accountant should also consider the applicability of existing pronouncements to new types of transactions or events that come to his attention.

Accounting Records Maintained at Multiple Locations

.13 In performing a review of interim financial information, considerations concerning locations to be visited for a client whose general accounting records are maintained at multiple locations ordinarily are similar to those involved in making an examination of the client's financial statements in accordance with generally accepted auditing standards. Usually this involves application of the foregoing procedures at both corporate headquarters and other locations selected by the accountant.

Questions Raised in Performing Other Procedures

.14 If, in performing a review of interim financial information, information comes to the accountant's attention that leads him to question whether the interim financial information to be reported conforms with generally accepted accounting principles, he should make additional inquiries or employ other procedures he considers appropriate to permit him to report on the interim financial information.

Modification of Review Procedures

.15 The procedures for a review of interim financial information may be modified, as appropriate, to take into consideration the results of auditing procedures applied in performing an examination in accordance with generally accepted auditing standards.

appendix
four

Regression Analysis in Analytical Review

The objective of this appendix is to present a brief, nontechnical introduction to regression analysis. It can be used as a nontechnical reference for auditors who are using regression analysis supplied, say, by a time-sharing vendor. Also, the auditor who is considering an initial use of regression analysis can study this material to obtain a better understanding of the benefits, limitations, and assumptions which are involved. There are a number of good references for a more complete, technical presentation, for example, J. Johnson, *Econometric Methods,* 2d ed., McGraw-Hill, New York, 1972. A good illustration of the use of regression analysis in auditing is presented in Alex W. Kask, "Regression and Correlation Analysis," *CPA Journal,* October 1979, pp. 35–41.

WHY REGRESSION?

The costs associated with using regression analysis are well known. There are the required expertise, additional data gathering, and unknown cost which can result from an improper use or interpretation of the analysis.

On the plus side, regression offers many advantages in the context of objectively and systematically quantifying the evidence available to the auditor. This means greater precision than can be obtained by nonstatistical methods. The precision derives from the fact that regression finds the best-fitting line through all data points. More importantly, the regression analysis provides measures of reliability and precision with each regression equation, so that the auditor has a direct and objective measure of the strength of the evidence. Further, the regression approach provides a rich modeling base for the auditor; it can accommodate two or more predictor variables if appropriate, and it can be modified to handle nonlinear relationships as well.

TYPES OF REGRESSION MODELS

As noted in Chapter 3, there are two fundamentally different types of regression models—the time-series model and the cross-sectional model. The former is fitted over data from many accounting periods (often 36 to 40 periods), whereas the latter is fitted from data from different locations or subunits of the organization at one point in time. Time-series analysis is the most commonly used in analytical review, though the cross-sectional method is useful for the "multiple location problem" described in Chapter 6.

HOW REGRESSION WORKS

Simple regression analysis is a statistical method for finding the best-fitting line for an equation of the form $y = a + bx + E$ through a given set of data points. The variable y is called the dependent variable, x is the independent variable, b is the coefficient of the independent variable, a is the intercept, and E is the error term.

We now show how regression works in a simple illustration involving only three data points wherein direct labor hours (x) is used to predict maintenance expense (y). We use only three data points for simplicity. Usually a regression will require 10 or more points to have satisfactory reliability, as we will see in the following section.

Maintenance Expense (y)	Direct Labor Hours (x)
$ 8.00	10
12.00	20
13.00	30

Regression analysis finds the unique straight line which minimizes the sum of the squared "errors," where an error is the difference between the actual value for the dependent variable and the predicted value from the regression model. This is shown in Figure A4-1, which plots the above data and shows the regression line which is derived from these data. The distances marked E in the figure are the error terms which, when squared, are minimized through the analysis to determine the best-fitting line. Note that the line cannot be shifted in any manner without increasing the sum of the squared errors. For this reason, the regression line is sometimes called the "least squares" regression line.

The distances indicated by T and M in the figure refer, respectively, to the "total" distance to be explained, and to the portion of the total distance which is explained by the model. In statistical language, the sum of E^2 is called the "error sum of squares," the sum of M^2 is called the "model sum of squares," and the sum of T^2 is referred to as the "total sum of squares." By construction, and as is apparent in Figure A4-1, the sum of M^2 + the sum of E^2 = the sum of T^2.

The three components of the "sum of squares" identified above are important in regression analysis. They form the basis for determining the measures of precision and reliability for the regression model. Here,

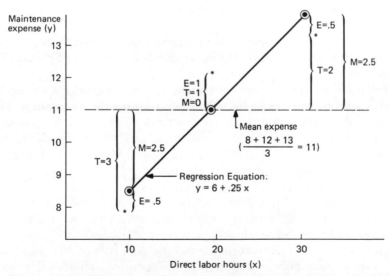

Figure A4-1 Illustration of hypothetical regression model to predict maintenance expense. *Key to figure:* asterisked coordinates (*) = actual values; circled coordinates = predicted values (on regression line); T = "total" distance = | actual value − mean |; E = "error" distance = | predicted value − actual value |; M = proportion of the distance "explained" by the model = | predicted value − mean |.

we are using these terms in a sense which is familiar to auditors. *Precision* refers to the width of the interval around an estimate within which the auditor can be confident the unknown true value will be. *Reliability* refers to the probability that the regression equation is not a quirk or accident, that is, the relationship between the dependent and independent variable or variables which is reflected in the equation exists in the real world.

MEASURES OF PRECISION AND RELIABILITY

In this section we describe six of the most important statistical measures provided by regression analysis:

1. R^2, the coefficient of determination
2. F, the F value
3. SE, the standard error of the estimate
4. SE_c, the standard error of the coefficient for the independent variable
5. t, the t value
6. DW, the Durbin-Watson statistic

Regression analysis is often accompanied by additional statistics, but the six measures above capture the most significant aspects of precision and reliability.

In order to explain these measures, we find the concept of the M, E, and T sum of squares to be useful. Reconsider the example in Figure A4-1. We compute the three components of the sum of squares and summarize the results in what is called an "analysis of variance table," as is shown in Table A4-1. This is a common format in which computer programs for regression present the output of the analysis.

The first column of Table A4-1 indicates the type of sum of squares. Any regression model, no matter how many data points or independent variables it has, will have the same three elements. Next, the sum of squares is computed as shown, based on the "distances" observed in Figure A4-1. The next column shows the "degrees of freedom," which represent the number of potential independent choices that can be made. The model degrees of freedom are always equal to the number of independent variables, in this case 1. The total degrees of freedom are always equal to the number of data points minus 1, in this case 2. And, the error degrees of freedom are the residual, the total degrees of freedom less the model degrees of freedom.

Table A4-1 Analysis of Variance Table for Data in Figure A4-1

Source of Sum of Squares	Sum of Squares	Degrees of Freedom	Mean Square	F
Model (M)	$12.5 = (2.5)^2 + (0)^2 + (2.5)^2$	1*	$12.5 = \dfrac{12.5}{1}$	$8.33 = \dfrac{12.5}{1.5}$
Error (E)	$1.5 = (.5)^2 + (1)^2 + (.5)^2$	1†	$1.5 = \dfrac{1.5}{1}$	
Total (T)	14.0	2‡		

$$R^2 = \frac{12.5}{14.0} = .893$$

$$SE = \sqrt{1.5} = 1.225$$

*Model degrees of freedom equal the number of independent variables, in this case 1.
†Error degrees of freedom are equal to total degrees of freedom minus model degrees of freedom.
‡Total degrees of freedom equal the number of data points minus 1, in this case, $3 - 1 = 2$.

The next column, mean square, is simply the ratio of the sum of squares to the degrees of freedom. And in the final column, the F value is the ratio of the mean square term for the model to the mean square error.

Now we are ready to see whence our six measures are derived and how they are interpreted. The first two, R^2 and F, address the reliability question.

$$R^2 = \frac{\text{sum of squares (model)}}{\text{sum of squares (total)}} = \frac{12.5}{14} = 0.893$$

R^2 is a direct measure of the explanatory power of the regression equation. In a sense, the regression "captures" or "explains" the variability in the dependent variable. If a change in the dependent variable can be explained or associated with a corresponding change in the independent variable by means of the regression line, then both the model sum of squares and R^2 should be relatively high. Values for R^2 range from 0 to 1; the closer R^2 is to 1, the better is the regression's explanatory power.

$$F = \frac{\text{mean square (model)}}{\text{mean square (error)}} = \frac{12.5}{1.5} = 8.33$$

The F value is a measure of the statistical validity of the model. Statistical validity can be interpreted as follows. Does the relationship between variables depicted in the model really exist? Or, is the regression result an artifact of a chance pattern to the data, wherein R^2 is really near zero? A large F value gives comfort that such is not the case. The actual size of

F needed for the auditor to conclude that the regression is not an artifact depends on the auditor's desired confidence level (usually 95 percent) and the number of degrees of freedom for the model and error mean square terms. These values are readily available in tabular form in statistics textbooks and reference books and are often included in the computer output of the regression model.

The F value and R^2 will usually be consistent and tell us the same thing. However, if the number of data points is very large (several hundred or more), then the model might have good statistical validity (high F) and at the same time have low explanatory power (low R^2). This effect is caused by the sample size having an influence on the denominator of the F value, while having no effect necessarily on the two components of R^2. The reverse would be true for very small samples. In both these situations the auditor must interpret the results carefully. Are both explanatory power and statistical validity acceptable for the model?

Together, the R^2 and F measures give the auditor an objective basis for judging the reliability of the regression model. If the model scores satisfactorily, the auditor can go ahead with the use of the model for prediction. If not, the auditor will want to modify the model or build a new one. At this time, the auditor should consider the following matters as a guide to developing a new model:

1. Have I modeled the underlying relationships properly? Are they linear or nonlinear? Additive or multiplicative?
2. Have I included all relevant independent variables in the model? Is the model complete?
3. Have I studied the data to identify any unusual data points or patterns to the data? Are the data clustered in an unusual manner? Are one or more points far removed from the others?

Each of the above potential problems can be addressed in the regression analysis to improve the fit of the model.

The next two of the six measures, SE and SE_C, can be used to evaluate the precision of the regression model. How accurate are its predictions?

$$SE = \sqrt{\text{Mean square error}} = \sqrt{1.5} = 1.225$$

The SE value is interpreted as the range of values around the prediction, using the model, wherein the auditor is approximately 67 percent confident that the unknown true value of the dependent variable lies. When SE is doubled, the value reflects an interval, both plus and minus around the model's prediction, wherein the auditor can be 95 percent confident that the unknown true value will lie.

The above interpretation is most appropriate when the auditor's prediction is near the mean of the independent variable. The reason for this is that the total sum of squares, which is used in regression analysis, is measured from the mean of the independent variable. This means that the precision associated with predictions from the regression model is best when the value of the independent variable is near its mean, and worst when the independent variable is far from its mean. The formula to correct SE when predicting far from the mean is given as follows:

$$SE \text{ (corrected)} = SE \sqrt{1 + \frac{1}{n} + \frac{(\hat{x} - \bar{x})^2}{SS_x}}$$

where   n = number of data points

$\hat{x}$ = value of independent variable for which prediction is desired

SS_x = sum of squares for independent variable

$$= \sum_{i=1}^{n} (x_i - \bar{x})^2$$

Note from the above equation that the corrected SE is minimized when $\bar{x}$ is near to $\hat{x}$, as you would expect. The effect of the difference between $\hat{x}$ and $\bar{x}$ on precision should not be overlooked, since to neglect it could cause the auditor to be substantially overconfident in the precision of a given prediction.

Another type of standard error, SE_c, is interpreted in a similar manner, but it applies to the coefficient of the independent variable rather than the prediction from the regression equation. SE_c is commonly provided in the output of regression analysis. A large SE_c value relative to the coefficient often indicates that the independent variable does not have a particularly close relationship to the dependent variable. In a simple regression with one independent variable, a large SE_c will ordinarily mean also a large SE value, with the result that the regression precision is low.

The final two of the six measures, t and the Durbin-Watson statistic (DW), provide information concerning the reliability of the model. The t value addresses the issue of whether the independent variable is a significant predictor, while DW is a signal of a potential nonlinear relationship in the data.

$$t = \frac{\text{coefficient of the independent variable}}{SE_c}$$

The t value is a measure of the statistical validity of the independent variable and, as such, is interpreted in much the same way as the F value.

A t value larger than approximately 2.0 is an indication that the independent variable has a significant statistical relationship with the dependent variable. Lower values suggest the relationship may not exist for these variables.

The DW statistic is a useful measure of the potential for a nonlinear relationship between the dependent and independent variable. Since regression is a linear method, it is important to know the extent of nonlinearity which might exist. If a nonlinear relationship is not detected, the *SE* values produced by the linear regression analysis will underestimate the true level of the standard error. As a result, the auditor will conclude there is greater precision of prediction than is warranted.

The DW statistic ranges from 0 to 4. A value between 1 and 3 would indicate no significant problem as described above. But, when *DW* is outside the 1 to 3 range, the auditor should reexamine the data to eliminate the nonlinearity by either adding independent variables, dropping variables, or transforming variables. A method which is often used for time-series data is to use the "first differences" in the variables, rather than the original data. The *first difference* is the amount of the change from period to period. First differences often eliminate the nonlinearity. We discuss transforming variables in more detail later.

ILLUSTRATIVE REGRESSION MODEL

This section presents a complete numerical illustration for a small regression problem. Those looking only for a overview of regression analysis may prefer to skip now to the next section.

The illustration we have chosen is the use of regression to predict maintenance expense on the basis of square feet of floor space. The analysis is done for seven retail outlets for which we have current maintenance expense and floor space data. These data are shown in the first three columns of Table A4-2. The audit objective might be to use the error terms from the regression as a basis for identifying problem outlets for further investigation.

Table A4-2 summarizes the computational aspects of the analysis. In this simple problem it is possible to show all the necessary arithmetic in a single table. For more complex problems involving more data or additional independent variables, the computer would be used to make these calculations.

The best way to understand Table A4-2 is to read it from the bottom

Table A4-2 Results for Illustrative Regression Analysis

Outlet	Maintenance Expense (y)	Square Feet of Floor Square (x)	x^2	xy	Regression Prediction (ŷ)	Error (E)	E^2
1	12	61	3721	732	11.994	.006	.0000
2	16	72	5184	1152	16.042	.042	.0018
3	18	75	5625	1350	17.146	.854	.7293
4	22	89	7921	1958	22.298	.298	.0888
5	19	80	6400	1520	18.986	.014	.0002
6	8	54	2916	432	9.418	1.418	2.0107
7	9	50	2500	450	7.946	1.054	1.1109
	$\Sigma y = 104$	$\Sigma x = 481$	$\Sigma x^2 = 34,267$	$\Sigma xy = 7594$			3.9417

$$(\Sigma x)^2 = (481)^2 = 231,361$$

$$a = \frac{(\Sigma y)(\Sigma x^2) - (\Sigma x)(\Sigma xy)}{n(\Sigma x^2) - (\Sigma x)^2} = \frac{(104)(34,267) - (481)(7594)}{(7)(34,267) - 231,361} = -\$10.454$$

$$b = \frac{(n)(\Sigma xy) - (\Sigma x)(\Sigma y)}{(n)(\Sigma x^2) - (\Sigma x)^2} = \frac{(7)(7594) - (481)(104)}{(7)(34,267) - 231,361} = .368$$

Regression equation: $y = -\$10.454 + .368x$

up. The regression equation obtained from the data is

Maintenance expense $= -\$10.454 + .368 \times$ square feet

The negative intercept looks suspicious, but is not a problem so long as we are using the regression to analyze the seven outlets only and do not extend our analysis beyond these outlets. More on this matter later.

Directly above the equation are the calculations needed to derive the intercept a and coefficient b of the equation. The data supporting these computations are at the top of the table.

The information in Table A4-2 can be used to develop an analysis of variance table. This is done in Table A4-3. The statistical measures are shown at the bottom of the table. These measures indicate a relatively reliable and precise model. R^2 and F are high, and the SE is low relative to the mean of the dependent variable. The auditor may then conclude that the planned use of the model will give meaningful results.

Since the audit objective is to identify outlets with potentially excessive maintenance expense, the best approach would be to select outlet 7 on the basis of its high error term. Maintenance expense is $1.054 greater than predicted by the regression model. Of course, a variety of other types of information would also be brought to bear in making this judgment—audit history, age or configuration of the outlets, and so on.

MULTIPLE REGRESSION (two or more independent variables)

Though we have discussed only the simple regression case thus far, the concepts we have developed apply also to the multiple regression case. One unique and important characteristic of the multiple regression model is the potential problem of multicollinearity between independent variables. Multicollinearity reflects the situation wherein two or more of the independent variables are not truly independent. The effect, like that of an unfavorable DW statistic, is that the auditor is likely to overestimate the degree of precision actually present in the model.

NONLINEAR REGRESSION

The auditor is not likely to encounter pure linear relationships in the real world. The common approach is to use a tight range of values for

Table A4-3 Analysis of Variance Table for Illustrative Regression Analysis

Source of Sum of Squares	Sum of Squares	Degrees of Freedom	Mean Square	F
Model (M)	164.912	1	164.912	209.3
Error (E)	3.942	5	0.788	
Total (T)	168.854	6		

$$R^2 = \frac{164.912}{168.854} = .977$$

$$SE = \sqrt{0.788} = 0.888$$

$$SE_c = \frac{SE}{\sqrt{\sum_{i=1}^{7} (x_i - \bar{x})^2}} = \frac{0.888}{\sqrt{1209.83}} = 0.026$$

$$t = \frac{.368}{0.026} = 14.15$$

the independent variables, so that within the given small range approximate linearity can be assumed. Alternatively, the auditor can add polynomial terms $(x^2, x^3, xy, \ldots)$ as new independent variables to capture the nonlinearity. Another option is to transform the data using a log transform, a power function, or an exponential function.

In some cases, the auditor wishes to build a model with two or more independent variables which are not additively (and therefore not linearly) related. For example, the auditor wishing to predict payroll expense P from data about hours worked per employee H, number of employees E, and average wage rate W is dealing with a multiplicative rather than an additive model.

$$P = H \times E \times W$$

To use regression on these data properly, the auditor must transform it to a linear form. A common approach is to use the log transform, which is additive.

$$\log P = \log H + \log E + \log W$$

The regression equation would be fitted using transformed data, and predictions would be obtained by applying the antilog to the regression predictions.

ASSUMPTIONS

We close this discussion of regression analysis with an identification of the most important assumptions involved in using it properly. The auditor should carefully evaluate each assumption in each regression application. Failure to do so will generally lead to overconfidence in the precision of predictions from the model, as noted above.

1. *Accurate data.* The data used to fit the model must be accurate, or the model and its statistics will be misspecified. Research has shown that even small errors can have a significant effect on the achieved precision of the model.

2. *Relevant range.* The auditor should not use the regression model outside the range of values which were used to fit it. The coefficients and statistics of the model are relevant only in that range. Additionally, to avoid the effects of nonlinearity, the auditor, in fitting the model, should pick a range of data that is reasonably tight.

3. *Linearity.* The auditor should evaluate whether the relationship under examination is linear and whether the independent variables truly combine in an additive or multiplicative manner. There are a variety of means for dealing with nonlinearity if it is present.

4. *Trend effect.* When using time-series data, the auditor should be alert to separate the following two aspects of the model—the relationship between dependent and independent variable and the trend effect influencing both variables. The significant effect of trend on most accounting data means that care should be taken in time-series regression. When using time-series data, the auditor should consider the following suggestions:

    a. Use monthly rather than annual data, and use no more than 36 periods or so.

    b. The effect of trend might be captured by adding additional independent variables to the model.

    c. Using "first differences" on the data may eliminate the trend effect.

5. *Inclusion of all relevant variables.* Is the model complete? Are there additional explanatory variables which can be used to help predict the dependent variable?

6. *Statistical properties of the errors.* The proper interpretation of the regression statistics requires that the error terms (E) be distributed in a certain manner. In statistical language, the errors must be independent, distributed normally, and show constant variance.

index

about the
authors

Edward Blocher and John J. Willingham collaborated on the research that led to this book while associates in the research group at Peat, Marwick, Mitchell & Co. Professor Blocher now teaches at the University of North Carolina, Chapel Hill, and serves on the editorial boards of *Auditing: A Journal of Practice and Theory* and *Advances in Accounting Research*.

Mr. Willingham is a partner in the research group at Peat, Marwick, Mitchell & Co. He is the coauthor (with D. R. Carmichael) of two highly successful texts, *Auditing Concepts and Methods* and *Perspectives in Auditing* (both from McGraw-Hill).